Conscientious Objection in Turkey

Series Editors: Victoria M. Basham and Sarah Bulmer

The Critical Military Studies series welcomes original thinking on the ways in which military power works within different societies and geopolitical arenas.

Militaries are central to the production and dissemination of force globally but the enduring legacies of military intervention are increasingly apparent at the societal and personal bodily levels as well, demonstrating that violence and war-making function on multiple scales. At the same time, the notion that violence is as an appropriate response to wider social and political problems transcends militaries: from private security to seemingly 'non-military' settings such as fitness training and schooling, the legitimisation and normalisation of authoritarianism and military power occur in various sites. This series seeks original, high-quality manuscripts and edited volumes that engage with such questions of how militaries, militarism and militarisation assemble and disassemble worlds touched and shaped by violence in these multiple ways. It will showcase innovative and interdisciplinary work that engages critically with the operation and effects of military power and provokes original questions for researchers and students alike.

Available Titles:

Resisting Militarism: Direct Action and the Politics of Subversion
Chris Rossdale

Making War on Bodies: Militarisation, Aesthetics and Embodiment in International Politics
Catherine Baker

Disordered Violence: How Gender, Race and Heteronormativity Structure Terrorism
Caron Gentry

Sex and the Nazi Soldier: Violent, Commercial and Consensual Contacts during the War in the Soviet Union, 1941–1945
Regina Mühlhäuser (translated by Jessica Spengler)

The Military–Peace Complex: Gender and Materiality in Afghanistan
Hannah Partis-Jennings

Politics of Impunity: Torture, the Armed Forces and the Failure of Transitional Justice in Brazil
Henrique Tavares Furtado

Conscientious Objection in Turkey: A Socio-legal Analysis of the Right to Refuse Military Service
Demet Çaltekin

Forthcoming:

Poetic Prosthetics: Contemporary Soldier Writing and the Limping Back from War
Ron Ben-Tovim

Beyond the Wire: The Cultural Politics of Veteran Narratives
Nick Caddick

The Gendered and Colonial Lives of Gurkhas in Private Security: From Military to Market
Amanda Chisholm

War and Militarisation: The British, Canadian and Dutch Invasion of Southern Afghanistan
Paul Dixon

Inhabiting No-Man's-Land: Army Wives, Gender and Militarisation
Alexandra Hyde

Mobilising China's One-Child Generation: Education, Nationalism and Youth Militarisation in the PRC
Orna Naftali

Martialling Peace: How the Peacekeeper Myth Legitimises Warfare
Nicole Wegner

Conscientious Objection in Turkey

A Socio-legal Analysis of the Right to Refuse Military Service

DEMET ASLI ÇALTEKİN

EDINBURGH
University Press

Edinburgh University Press is one of the leading university presses in the UK. We publish academic books and journals in our selected subject areas across the humanities and social sciences, combining cutting-edge scholarship with high editorial and production values to produce academic works of lasting importance. For more information visit our website: edinburghuniversitypress.com

© Demet Aslı Çaltekin, 2022, 2024

Edinburgh University Press Ltd
The Tun – Holyrood Road
12(2f) Jackson's Entry
Edinburgh EH8 8PJ

First published in hardback by Edinburgh University Press 2022

Typeset in 10.5/13 ITC Giovanni Std by
IDSUK (DataConnection) Ltd

A CIP record for this book is available from the British Library

ISBN 978-1-4744-9649-0 (hardback)
ISBN   978-1-4744-9650-6 (paperback)
ISBN 978-1-4744-9651-3 (webready PDF)
ISBN 978-1-4744-9652-0 (epub)

CONTENTS

ACKNOWLEDGEMENTS

I owe a deep debt of gratitude to Professor Ian Leigh for being extraordinarily supportive during my time at Durham University, Law School, where this book started its journey. I am also indebted to Professor Deirdre McCann for her continuous academic and personal support. Her insightful and helpful suggestions paved the way for the publication of this book.

I would like to thank Majken Jul Sørensen and Jørgen Johansen for inviting me to use their rich library in Irene Publishing's Writers' Residence in Sweden while developing my interview questions. I cannot imagine more gracious hosts and more efficient assistance. The book also benefited from the valuable feedback that I received from conferences, particularly the American Association of Geographers Annual Meeting (in Chicago), Pan-European Conference on International Relations (Prague and Giardini Naxos), and Conference on Gender and Security in Violent Conflict – The Leonard Davis Institute for International Relations (Jerusalem).

I would also like to thank the editors of Advances in Critical Military Studies series, Sarah Bulmer and Victoria Basham, for their rich feedback, and the editorial team of Edinburgh University Press, mainly Ersev Ersoy and Gillian Leslie, for their support.

I am grateful to all my participants for sharing their experiences with me. Without their generous contributions, this research would not have followed the path it took. I hope the book manages to do justice to their narratives, enthusiasm and energy.

I am privileged to be a friend to the individuals whose many-faceted skills have been a source of inspiration and cheerful support. All of them contributed to this project in different ways. Some have read and commented on draft chapters, whereas others have offered me the comfort of companionship. It would be impossible to name them all but a few cannot escape mention: Semra Akay, Fahad Alhammadi, Raihana Ferdous, Vili Grigorova, Arin Mizouri and Esma Okur.

I am always blessed to find support from my family. I cannot imagine more caring sisters than Filiz, Canan and Hacer. The smiles of the two Denizes, Çınar and Arya, my nephews and niece, warmed my heart and enabled me to continue working. I am also thankful to my partner, Yazid Haroun, for being there for me and finding ways to make me laugh during stressful times.

LIST OF LEGISLATION

Domestic Legislation

1982 Constitution of the Republic of Turkey, Act No. 2709,
7 November 1982
1961 Turkish Constitution, Act No. 334, 9 July 1961
Law on Military Service, Act No. 1111, 20 March 1927
Military Penal Code, Act No. 1632, 22 May 1930
Turkish Armed Forces' Health Aptitude Regulations, No. 86/11092,
8 October 1986
Turkish Penal Code, Amended Law No. 5237, 26 September 2004
Turkish Penal Code, No. 765, 1 March 1926

International and Regional Treaties

European Convention on Human Rights, 3 September 1953
International Covenant on Civil and Political Rights, 19 December
1966

LIST OF CASES

Turkey Domestic Case Law

Enver Aydemir, Eskisehir Military Court, Case No. 2013/164, Decision No. 2013/349 (5 July 2013)

Muhammed Serdar Delice, Malatya Military Court, Case No. 2012/98, Decree No. 2012/40 (24 February 2012)

International and Regional Case Law

European Human Rights Law

Acik and Others v. Turkey App. No. 31451/03 (ECtHR, 13 January 2009)

Arrowsmith v. the United Kingdom App. No. 7050/75 (European Commission on Human Rights, 5 December 1978)

Bayatyan v. Armenia App. No. 23459/03 (ECtHR, 27 October 2009)

Bayatyan v. Armenia Grand Chamber App. No. 23459/03 (ECtHR, 7 July 2011)

Campbell and Cosans v. the United Kingdom App. Nos. 7511/76; 7743/76 (ECtHR, 25 February 1982)

Chappell v. United Kingdom App. No. 12587/86 (1987)

Darby v. Sweden App. No. 11581/85 (ECtHR, 23 October 1990)

Duzgoren v. Turkey App. No. 56827/00 (ECtHR, 9 November 2006)

Efstratiou v. Greece App. No. 24095/94 (ECtHR, 18 December 1996)

Engel and Others v. the Netherlands App. Nos. 5100/71; 5101/71; 5102/71; 5354/72; 5370/72 (ECtHR, 8 June 1976)

Ercep v. Turkey App. No. 43965/04 (ECtHR, 22 November 2011)

Ergin v. Turkey App. No. 47533/99 (ECtHR, 4 May 2006)

Eweida and Others v. the UK App. Nos. 48420/10, 59842/10, 51671/10 and 36516/10 (ECtHR 27 May 2013)

Setting the Scene: Militarisation of Society

My friend, you would not tell with such high zest
To children ardent for some desperate glory,
The old Lie: *Dulce et decorum est*
Pro patria mori.

(Wilfred Owen, quoted in Bloom 2002: 20)

When I was at primary school, I stood up every morning with all the other students and recited the national pledge of allegiance: 'I offer my existence to the Turkish nation as a gift.'[1] At Friday ceremonies, just before leaving the school, I read the national anthem of Turkey and burst out: 'Smile upon my heroic nation! Why the anger, why the rage? Our blood which we shed for you shall not be worthy otherwise.'[2] It is hardly surprising, outside school, that I felt the urge to behave like a soldier whenever I encountered one, giving them a military salute. These seemingly trivial practices (signs of normalisation of militarism) encouraged me to question the normalisation of the military's presence in our daily lives. It was during my LLM that I first studied the limitations on the right to freedom of expression on the grounds of maintaining national security, so as to scrutinise the impacts of militarism on individuals' freedom. My interest in investigating such impacts further led me to investigate how militarism is normalised but also resisted by conscientious objectors.

Resistance to the normalisation of militarism has been the main concern of critical military studies, and academics have recently started looking into conscientious objection in the context of Turkey. Some studies on conscientious objection in Turkey approach objection as a tool used to reject imposed hegemonic masculinity and gender stereotypes (see, for example, Aktas 2014). Others provide a legal analysis of the right to conscientious objection, investigating international standards on the legal recognition of the right to conscientious objection and offering domestic interpretations of the right to conscientious objection. However, they look at the issue from the legal perspective only and attempt to explain the militarisation of society using secondary sources[3] (see, for example, Çınar 2013; 2014). This book, the first socio-legal research on the matter, aims instead to reveal the social and cultural circumstances influencing the law, and to locate the law on conscientious objection and compulsory military service within socio-legal studies. It studies a sociological problem, considering its impact on law and vice versa, thus bringing a socio-legal perspective to critical military studies. This also entails an empirical investigation into the experiences of antimilitarists with law. To understand how the socio-cultural structure of a given society and its laws on conscription and resistance reciprocate, one cannot simply examine the legal texts on paper but must instead investigate empirically how such laws operate within society: more specifically, how the current legal framework affects the lives of conscientious objectors. Without an empirical focus, antimilitarist researchers risk detaching themselves from the real world. In light of this, the book provides empirical insights into how conscientious objectors experience the (non-)recognition of the right to conscientious objection. It approaches the problems pertaining to the current legal framework for military service from the personal experiences of conscientious objectors with the militarist system.

The book also aims to shed light on the social factors contributing to the non-recognition of the right to conscientious objection at the national level by asking 'how' and 'why' questions.[4] Why is the presence of the military in our daily routine unquestionable and how is the militarisation of society normalised in Turkey? Why does Turkey insist on non-recognition of the right to conscientious objection? How are those pursuing their conscience affected by such non-recognition? These questions are important as the law not only is shaped by the socio-cultural structures in which it operates but also (re)shapes these structures by bringing new perspectives into the matter and by framing perceptions of people. Therefore, any attempt to create social change also necessitates understanding and challenging the legal framework. In this light, the book argues that one cannot fully understand and, as a result, resist the militarisation of society without understanding the relationship between the law and social norms.

The Conscription System and the Normalisation of Militarism in Turkey

The introduction of the conscription system in 1927 provided fertile ground for the normalisation of militarism in Turkey. Compulsory military service precipitated debates on the necessities for having mass standing armies. Initially, justification for the conscription system was related to the need to protect the nation against any threats, 'existing' or potential. But then, the myths of 'Every Turk is born a soldier' and 'The Turkish nation is a military nation' became the most appealing justifications for the conscription system. Military service was no longer only a necessity but became a cultural characteristic of Turks. Such valorisation of military service left a lasting impact on education and is echoed in street or school names (Altınay 2004: 13). For instance, the military duty is defined in textbooks as follows:

> the principal task is to preserve and advance the Turkish motherland, independence and republic under all circumstances and provide the security of the Turkish nation. For this task to be accomplished [the individual] must be in the strongest possible bodily and spiritual state, devoted to one's duty with awareness and full of love for the country [. . .] Military discipline is a continuation and maturation of family discipline, school discipline and finally community discipline. Today the behaviour of a father who does not give his daughter to a man who has not fulfilled his military service is a reflection of the importance and value we, as a nation, place in the military and in military discipline. (cited in Aydın 2009: 29–30)

In this passage, military service is considered a cultural condition for a man to become a better citizen: to learn how to be strong and spiritual. Such an understanding reinforces the assumption that being a good citizen means, first and foremost, being a good soldier. Military service was believed not only to prepare young people for life by turning them into physically and spiritually strong individuals, but also to educate them, particularly those coming from rural areas, in line with modern and Western values. This is reflected in public speeches on the role of the army:

> While saving the very country, these soldiers also destroyed the political structure that had been based on the sultanate and caliphate [. . .] they built up a new, modern system based on societal power. This change was as important for Turkey as was the Renaissance for those in the West, and it was led by

soldiers. (speech by Hilmi Özkök, 24th Chief of General Staff between 2002 and 2006, cited in Aydinli et al. 2006: 2)

The passage illustrates how, since the establishment of the Republic, the Turkish military's ultimate aim was westernising the country. In thus constructing the Turkish Armed Forces (TAF), the founder of the Turkish Republic, as guardian of the new, modern and westernised country, also laid the basis for the contemporary militarisation process in Turkey. Turkey's social and political structure, which perceives Turks as warriors and the military as the school of the nation, enabled the military to interfere in politics and blurred the line between civilian and military spheres. Over time, the military's area of influence expanded from protecting the nation against enemies to guarding the democracy. Such an expansion made an indelible impression on society's perception of the military (Sakallioğlu 1997; Cizre 2011; Narli 2009a; 2009b; Aydinli et al. 2006) and, by extension, on the legal recognition of the right to conscientious objection. Under such circumstances, any critique pertaining to the military is perceived as a threat to the nation's existence and its spirit.

Conscientious Objection and Civil Disobedience: The Conflict Between Law and Conscience

Conscientious objection to military service is the product of a conflict between individuals' conscience, thought and belief and the law compelling them to join the army. Such a conflict raises controversial questions over the responsibilities of states in accommodating different forms of moral beliefs. Given the difficulties in assessing people's moral convictions, it becomes difficult for states to reach a consensus on responding to such a conflict (Greenawalt 1991: 174). The recognition and implementation of the right to conscientious objection differ between countries, despite the standards set by international and regional bodies: that is, Turkish domestic law conflicts with the conscientious objectors' right to religion, conscience and thought. Consequently, objectors run the risk of facing a series of criminal convictions, which subject them to 'civil death'. They are also deprived of their right to freedom of expression following Article 318 of the Turkish Penal Code, entitled 'alienating people from military service',[5] as this article penalises both objectors and their supporters (Üçpınar 2009: 248), and limits the 'critical media reporting' on public issues.[6]

The conflict between moral and legal obligations requires individuals to determine whether their conscience allows them to obey the law.

Their disobedience is not a threat to the legitimacy of the system; it is a 'way of manoeuvring between these conflicting moralities' (Walzer 1970: 24). Dissenters disobey because of the conflict they experience between political or legal circumstances and their deepest moral convictions. The act of civil disobedience, then, naturally involves conscientious grounds (Bedau 1961: 659). This makes it difficult to provide a comprehensive definition of civil disobedience or to reach an agreement on whether the authorities should distinguish between ordinary criminals and law-breakers with a conscientious reason. Its scope, therefore, remains ambiguous (Bedau 1991: 49).

John Rawls (1999: 320) defines civil disobedience 'as a public, non-violent, conscientious yet political act contrary to law usually done with the aim of bringing about a change in the law or policies of the government'. For Rawls (1999: 320), '[b]y acting in this way one addresses the sense of justice of the majority of the community and declares that in one's considered opinion the principles of social cooperation among free and equal men are not being respected'. Rawls limits the scope of civil disobedience to acts intending to invoke the 'majority's shared conception of justice'. He also believes civil disobedience cannot be justified by principles of personal morality or by religious doctrines. Rawls's conceptualisation of civil disobedience overlooks the fact that inner convictions, in some cases, motivate dissenters to create an environment in which they can live in harmony with their personal motivations. This point applies to conscientious objection to military service in Turkey, where objectors consider their objection as part of a movement and locate their argument within a discussion of war, militarism, patriarchy and so on. For this reason, categorising their objection as a 'merely' private act would have detrimental impacts on the legitimacy of their wider demands. Such a categorisation would also reduce the scope of the right to conscientious objection to a merely personal exemption. Given this, the book pays attention to the objectors' demands for societal change and forges a link between civil disobedience and conscientious objection.

Conscientious Objection and Gender

Gender shapes institutions, culture and social practices. It creates the best environment for maintaining and strengthening militarism (Woodward and Winter 2007: 3). As Cynthia Enloe (2007: 11) also argues, 'militaristic ideas are so deeply imbued with gendered assumptions and values'. The gendered understanding within the military institution is reflected in society, particularly in highly militarised societies, where becoming a soldier is considered the highest virtue (Duncanson 2015: 232). In view of that, this book examines the role of gender in the normalisation of militarism by adopting Enloe's (2004: 220) feminist curiosity – a curiosity that encourages us to challenge what is considered natural and trivial. By adopting Enloe's feminist curiosity, the book tries to make sense of women's conscientious objection to military service in the male conscription system. Yet, as Enloe (2009: 81) argues, 'the use of a feminist curiosity to fully understand conscientious objection means going further, exploring women's full range of relationships to men, to ideas of manliness and to soldiering and militaristic cultures in general'. Therefore, to understand gender relations, it is necessary to consider the relationship between men and women rather than limiting the critique of manhood to the hierarchy among men and adopting a 'feminist perspective' which focuses only on women (Cockburn and Žarkov 2002: 14–15). In this respect, the book examines how male objectors perceive women's involvement in the movement by focusing on the relationship between masculinity and militarism.

Male-conscription systems sustain their 'effectiveness' through the strong relationship between military service and masculinity. The military's male-dominated structure, even in the era of volunteering, is yet another example showing the relationship between military service and masculinity (Moon 2005: 65). Indeed, not all men reach the same level in the hierarchy chain, though masculinity allows men to reach the top, as opposed to women. That is, not all masculinities enjoy the same 'privileges' or suffer the same 'pain' (Dowd et al. 2011). R. W. Connell's hegemonic masculinities concept refers to this hierarchy and subordination among different kinds of masculinities. For Connell (2005: 77), 'hegemony is likely to be established only if there is some correspondence between cultural ideal and institutional power, collective if not individual. So, the top levels of business, the military and government provide a fairly convincing corporate display of masculinity.' This means that socially accepted masculine norms dominate and occupy a position at the top of the hierarchy promoted by institutions, such as militaries.

Fieldwork[7]

As Kjell Skjelsbaek (1979) argues, militarism is shaped within a specific time and space; thus, it is difficult to provide a unitary definition of it. As a result, Skjelsbaek views militarism as a set of diseases and so tries to understand the symptoms rather than giving a definition. In a similar vein, this book attempts to understand the motivations behind the conscientious objectors' refusal and their daily life experiences that shed light on the multi-layered aspects of the militarisation process – the symptoms. The book aims to unveil the reasons that are conducive to conscientious objection. It draws on data collected from semi-structured interviews with eighteen objectors (eight women and ten men) and a single expert, conducted in June and July 2016 in Ankara and Istanbul. Although the participants share some common points of view on militarisation, their unique life stories, their understanding of militarism and the driving force behind their aim to reverse militarism differ markedly. In this sense, the semi-structured interviews allowed me to comprehend the experiences and perspectives of individuals affected by militarism and cover the objectors' unique stories, understand their encounter with militarism and make sense of the multi-dimensional nature of their refusal.

Turkey is the only member of the Council of Europe that has not recognised the right to conscientious objection. Since the country still adopts the male-conscription system, antimilitarists challenge militarism and gendered relations by refusing compulsory military service. They use conscientious objection as a political tool to challenge the militarisation of society. They aim to bring about change in the gendered and militarised society and to question the militarisation of everyday life. The number of conscientious objectors in Turkey is increasing. Since there is no legal procedure for conscientious objection, there is no official information on the number of objectors. The only data available come from the Association of Conscientious Objection in Turkey, which, according to its website, has around 543 members. To provide an updated analysis of the movement in this research, I tried to reach those conscientious objectors who are actively involved in the movement by using snowballing sampling. I selected interviewees by using snowballing sampling as it allows the interviewee to direct the researcher's attention to other potential interviewees (Ritchie 2011: 94). I reached them through the personal connections of two objectors, Atlas Arslan in Ankara and Ercan Jan Aktaş in Istanbul. Of the eight women objectors, ten men objectors and a single expert interviewed, seventeen identified themselves as anarchists while one held no political views. Fifteen interviewees considered their objection as political, two of them as both religious and political, and one as humanistic. The interviewees had various occupations: seven students, one theatre actor, four journalists, one social worker, one self-employed person, one waitress, two lawyers and one veterinarian. They were members of the Association of Conscientious Objection and activists working on war, gender and militarism. Although they were given the option to remain anonymous, none of them asked for anonymity[8] because they publicly and consistently refuse the call-ups and most of them are known public figures. Since they are not deserters but rather objectors, they had no intention of hiding their identity.

It is important to clarify that snowball sampling carries the risk of 'overrepresentation of a single, networked group' (Harrell and Bradley 2009: 31). It prevents researchers from reaching diverse segments of society. For instance, during the interviews, almost all of respondents answered my question on 'how did your friends react to your objection?' by emphasising that their friend circle is isolated from militarised and gendered minds, or that they are surrounded by people who share similar views. Yet, even though the interviewees were a homogeneous group coming from Kurd, Alevi, secular, middle-class backgrounds, their families' reaction differed considerably. While some of the participants believed that their family did not understand them, others experienced family support, or at least believed that they had made their voices heard. Furthermore, I reached members of the same group, particularly anarchists and members of the Association of Conscientious Objection. I could not reach those already serving in the army, mainly to avoid any possible prosecutions. Indeed, each case study has its limitations and boundaries. 'The "case" must carry with it some idea of a boundary which is sufficiently clear and obvious to allow the researcher to see what is contained within the case' (Denscombe 2003: 37–8).

It is also essential to address issues related to the self-involvement of the researcher. As Martyn Denscombe (2010: 302) suggests, 'the researcher's identity, values and beliefs play a role in the production and analysis of qualitative data and therefore researchers should come clean about the way their research agenda has been shaped by personal experiences and social backgrounds'. There are two approaches to the matter. The first argues that researchers should distance themselves from interviewees and 'adopt a passive neutral stance' (Denscombe 2010: 179). The second claims that 'a cold and calculating style of interviewing reinforces a gulf between the researcher and the informant, and does little to help or empower the informant' (Denscombe 2010: 180). Researchers should engage in a constructive dialogue instead of being distant. Such a dialogue also allows researchers to observe whether interviewees 'understand and share the underlying logic of the approach' (Denscombe 2010: 180). The position taken in this book is a combination of these two approaches. During my fieldwork in Turkey, sharing similar experiences with some of the interviewees provided me with an opportunity to create an environment in which they felt comfortable enough to elaborate on the interview questions in detail. At the same time, I knew I was a complete stranger to them at the beginning, so I avoided personal and sensitive questions. Also, to create a non-biased environment, I refrained from making negative, discouraging and misleading comments. I informed the interviewees about the aim of the research in a manner that did not elicit a particular response. Furthermore, I observed how they reacted when I introduced myself and my research topic, in order to see how approachable they were. While I engaged in emotional and personal dialogues with some objectors, with others I interfered only to guide the interview.

Structure of the Book

The book is composed of six chapters. Chapter 1 seeks to examine the militarisation of society and provides the sociological background to the conscription system in Turkey. It first examines the historical role of the TAF in politics and everyday life to understand the roots of the problem at a national level. The chapter scrutinises the institutionalised power of the military, its role in shaping society through soft means, and the cultural and social practices viewing the military as a sacred institution. It also provides a gender analysis of compulsory military service, with a particular focus on the exclusion of women. The chapter then reconsiders civil–military relations in light of the socio-political changes in Turkey during the Justice and Development Party era, with a particular focus on, first, the institutional changes brought in with the European Union (EU) harmonisation packages, and second, social change after the 15 July 2016 coup attempt. The chapter mainly argues that despite the decreasing role of the TAF at the institutional level and the fact that society's perceptions have changed, militarism is still omnipresent in contemporary Turkey.

Chapters 2 and 3 examine the legal background to conscientious objection. Chapter 2 analyses the legal status of conscientious objection at international and regional levels. It focuses on the conflict between conscience and law, which raises controversial questions over the responsibility of states in accommodating different forms of moral beliefs. It attempts to answer the question of whether the right to religion, conscience and thought constitutes a legal ground for claiming the right to conscientious objection. In this context, it first examines the right to religion, conscience and thought in the light of the European Convention on Human Rights (ECHR) and the case law of the European Court of Human Rights (ECtHR). Moreover, in the light of Article 14 of the ECHR (protection from discrimination), it analyses the unequal treatment received by conscientious objectors with criminal records. Therefore, it aims to answer the question of whether failing to distinguish conscientious objectors from other law-breakers violates Article 14 of the ECHR. The chapter then analyses the right to conscientious objection under the International Covenant on Civil and Political Rights (ICCPR) and the case law of Human Rights Committee (HRC). The chapter adopts the right to freedom of thought, conscience and religion as the main legal ground for recognition of the right to conscientious objection in order to study the obstacles faced by objectors.

Having analysed international standards on the right to conscientious objection in Chapter 2, I explore in Chapter 3 whether Turkey's domestic law – that is, Article 318 of the Penal Code, entitled 'alienating people from military service' – is compatible with international standards. The chapter examines significant domestic cases to understand the current legal problems of conscientious objection under domestic Turkish law. In this context, it focuses on the criminalisation of objection ('civil death'), with particular attention paid to Turkey's compliance with international standards on the following key aspects: the right to freedom of expression, the arbitrary detention of conscientious objectors, the prohibition of torture, and inhuman and degrading treatment.

Chapters 4, 5 and 6 examine the sociology of resistance in Turkey. Chapter 4 discusses the different forms of conscientious objection to military service. It investigates the socio-economic background of the interviewees, their political views, age and occupation, and their family's response to their objection. Therefore, it sheds light on how conscientious objection is understood in this book. Chapter 5 studies the nature of conscientious objection and its relationship with civil disobedience. It examines the conflict between conscience and law. To clarify whether conscientious objection to military service is an act of civil disobedience, it utilises Charles Moskos and Whiteclay Chambers's classification of conscientious objection and John Rawls's definition of civil disobedience. It contributes to the current philosophical debate on civil disobedience by providing empirical evidence on the differences and similarities between civil disobedience and conscientious objection in Turkey. It argues that a conscientiously motivated act – namely, conscientious objection to military service – could form a collective act that aims to bring about a change in society. Such an aim inevitably leads objectors to challenge the gendered roots of militarism. Therefore, Chapter 6, utilising Cynthia Enloe's feminist curiosity, provides empirical evidence to show how the link between militarism, gender and conscientious objection is understood and challenged in Turkey, where women are not conscripted yet they declare their conscientious objection. It explores the impacts of militarism on women and offers a picture of women's demilitarisation attempts in Turkey. It illustrates how conscription constitutes only a single dimension of militarism and how militarism also affects women's lives, even though they are not subject to compulsory military service. Therefore, by studying curious women conscientious objectors in the male-conscription system, this chapter approaches conscientious objection from a wider perspective and broadens the discussion on the right to conscientious objection by studying those who have previously been assumed to be 'irrelevant'.

The concluding chapter presents the book's findings, highlights its contribution and exposes its limitations. It offers recommendations for possible legal reforms in Turkey. It provides the following conclusion: an explicit and inclusive recognition of the right to conscientious objection, accepting absolute, total and political forms of objection, will bring an end to human rights violations. It is noteworthy that the demilitarisation of society, like militarism itself, is an on-going struggle that cannot be reduced merely to the rejection of compulsory military service. Conscientious objection is a tool which makes gendered and militarist structures visible. Therefore, legal recognition of the right to conscientious objection would be just one piece in the puzzle. To complete the puzzle, objectors will continue resisting different appearances of gendered and militarist structures in our daily life in different ways.

Notes

1. 'On 8 September 2013, the *Official Gazette* announced that the practice of reciting the Student Oath was abolished.' For the wording, see <https://en.wikipedia.org/wiki/Student_Oath_(Turkey)#History_of_the_Student_Oath> (last accessed 3 January 2022).
2. For the lyrics, see <https://en.wikipedia.org/wiki/%C4%B0stiklal_Mar%C5%9F%C4%B1#Lyrics> (last accessed 3 January 2022).
3. Hadar Aviram, in her review of Çınar's work, indicates that 'I found myself, however, wishing for considerably less doctrine and considerably more socio-legal analysis of sources for Turkey's noncompliance. Çınar's discussion of nation building and militarization is based on secondary sources, which was disappointing given that it was the most interesting part of the book' (Aviram 2015).
4. In line with Robert Yin's argument that 'case studies are the preferred strategy when "how" or "why" questions are being posed' (Yin 1994).
5. Article 318 reads as follows: 'People who urge those carrying out their military service to desert or suggest to those who are yet to carry out their military service

to be dissuaded from carrying it out are imprisoned for six months to two years' (The New Turkish Penal Code Amended Law No. 5237, 26 September 2004, Article 318).

6. United Nations Human Rights Committee, 'Concluding Observations on the Initial Report of Turkey Adopted by the Committee at Its 106th Session 15 October to 2 November (13 November 2012) CCPR/C/TUR/CO/1' para.24.

7. To comply with Durham University regulations, I applied for ethical approval in February 2016 before conducting the interviews. My application was sent to Durham Business School's Sub-Committee for Ethics and I received formal approval in March 2016; the interviews were all conducted between April and May 2016.

8. This matter was explained to the Ethics Committee at Durham University before ethical approval was granted, the Committee approving my request for displaying interviewees' names.

CHAPTER 1

Conscription and Turkey's Changing Socio-political Structures

Introduction

The sources of present beliefs are past experiences and practices [. . .]
Prior institutions, prior strategies, prior actions delimit current opinions,
and stories of yesteryear reveal what bargains have been broken and which
kept [. . .] History also shapes institutions and regimes, and history can reveal
the underlying causes for institutional change or stability.

(Levi 1997: 3)

Significant historical events that change societies do not happen in a
vacuum. They involve lengthy processes of convincing people to embrace
the new conditions. The introduction of the conscription system is
undoubtedly one of those processes that required a long persuasion
phase. Hence, historical facts behind the emergence of the conscription
system and the gradual integration of military values into society reveal
the core beliefs influencing the conscription system in general and
unveil the tools used by states to gain society's consent. History does
indeed mirror states' policies regarding the conscription system and
offers valuable insights into the perspectives and motivations of those
opposing conscription.

Historically, conscription during war was seen as the most efficient
system to boost manpower, strengthen national identity and enforce the
notion of the good citizen (Burk 1992: 50). The 'victory' of the armies
further provides justification for having a conscription system and mass
armies. Turkey was not immune to this perception of 'victory'. The trau-
matic effects of two big wars, World War I and the War of Independence,
had an immense effect on shaping the conscription system in Turkey
and society's perception of compulsory military service. When the War

of Independence brought about victory, the TAF gained social support and were hailed as the 'hero' (Celenk 2009: 123). Since the creation of the new Republic, the Armed Forces have continued to play a significant role in the political arena because they contributed to the Republic-building process and the westernising of society. This turned the army into a 'political symbol of nationhood' and a tool used to maintain national security (Sakallioğlu 1997, 154). Even after the establishment of the Republic, the top figures involved in politics continued to have a military background, and Mustafa Kemal Atatürk, founder of the Republic, enjoyed the military's support for the reforms and principles that he introduced (Tachau and Heper 1983: 19–20). In the new Republic, only one attempt was made by Atatürk to separate politicians from soldiers, when he asked military members of parliament to choose between being soldiers or politicians in a public speech:

> Commanders should avoid the effects of politics while they are fulfilling their duties as soldiers. They should remember that there are people who will fulfil the political obligations. The separation of army from politics is an important principle of the Republic. (cited in Celenk 2009: 122)

Although this institutional separation is seen as an important step towards reducing any tendentious interference of military officials in politics (Turan 1997: 125–6), it was not directed at enabling civilian control of the military (Sakallioğlu 1997: 156). Despite this separation attempt, the military remained powerful enough to influence the political situation (Turan 1997: 126). Atatürk, indeed, insisted that the Commander of the Armed Forces, Marshal Fevzi Cakmak, must be in the Cabinet and serve as Prime Minister. These conditions considered, it can be said that there were no real attempts to separate the military from the civilian sphere. Military officers were part of the Cabinet and actively involved in politics (Harris 1965: 54–5).

The way that Turkish society embraces such an integration of the army into the civilian sphere and its perception of military service have significant impacts on recognition of the right to conscientious objection. Society's stance on compulsory military service has contributed to prevailing justifications for having a standing army. For this reason, even though domestic law in Turkey does not recognise the right to conscientious objection as a human right, debates on the legal dimensions of the right to conscientious objection itself are insufficient alone to analyse the military's influence on society. To understand the current legal framework on recognition of the right to conscientious objection in Turkey, one must highlight the influence of the army on politics and education, and also the cultural aspects of military service, including social practices as symbols and beliefs. Therefore, this chapter examines civil–military relations by considering the sociological factors that turn the military into an unquestionable and sacred institution. It seeks to examine the militarisation of society and provide the sociological background for the conscription system in Turkey. It first examines the concept of national security, and then scrutinises the institutionalised power of the military, its role in shaping society through soft means, and the cultural and social practices that view the military as a sacred institution. The chapter also reconsiders civil–military relations in light of the socio-political changes in Turkey during the Justice and Development Party era, with a particular focus, first, on the institutional changes brought in with the EU harmonisation packages, and second, social change after the attempted coup of 15 July 2016. The chapter mainly argues that despite the decreasing role of the TAF at an institutional level and the fact that society's perception has changed, militarism is still omnipresent in contemporary Turkey.

Why Have a Standing Army?

War is likely to produce large armies comprised of volunteers. It has psychological impacts on citizens, compelling them to participate in the war effort. However, mass standing armies are the product of conscription systems. As Jacques van Doorn (1975: 149–50) correctly notes, 'the mass army is quite rightly seen in relation to the draft'. However, serving in the army carries heavy burdens, such as using lethal weapons, 'killing and dying', and obeying orders (Frevert 2004: 2). Justifying these burdens and the idea of having a standing army during peacetime compels states to enter a process of conviction. In Turkey, with the impact of World War I and the War of Independence, the necessity to protect national security played a significant role in gaining society's approval and legitimising certain institutional practices. Significant importance is attributed to the concept of national security, one that is considered by Ümit Cizre Sakallioğlu (1997: 154) as a kind of 'obsessive anxiety'. The military's influence on the political situation and on society at large has been legitimised by the concept of national security, which is defined in vague and broad terms. Although it is frequently mentioned in Turkish law, 'national security' has no clear definition[1] (Urhan and Çelik 2010: 11). National security discourse, therefore, plays an important role in both the recognition of the right to conscientious objection and the expansion of the dominant position of the Turkish military.

Political and legal structures have considerable impact on the selection of actors who define national security (Celenk 2009: 120). In Turkey, the 'definition of security has been more in military than non-military terms' (Cizre 2007: 5). Also, as underlined by Pınar Bilgin (2007: 558), the definition of the national security concept 'does not depend on objective criteria but on the relevant actors'. Such actors have the power to include any issue deemed necessary to the national security agenda. However, conceptualising national security through the lens of the military not only positions the army as the main actor capable of defining national security but also grants military institutions supremacy over civilian institutions (Celenk 2009: 120–1).

Maintaining national security in Turkey is considered as 'being able to have capabilities and opportunities if there is a need' (Ustun and Senyuva 2013: 273). The excessive concern over having a standing army, always ready to face enemies, is justified by Turkey's geographical position, and politicians have adopted national security policies based on the idea that external enemies surround the country. According to former President Kenan Evren, 'Turkey's historical position indicates that it is obliged to pursue a policy based on being strong and stable within its region [. . . since] it is surrounded by unfriendly neighbours' (cited in Ustun and Senyuva 2013: 273). A speech by the Commander of the Military Academy, delivered at the military school, also shows how politicians have expressed concerns over Turkey's geographical position:

> You will see that Turkey has the most internal and external enemies of any country in the world. You will learn about the dirty aspirations of those who hide behind values such as democracy and human rights and who want to take revenge on the Republic of Atatürk. (cited in Bilgin 2005: 184)

Overemphasising Turkey's geographical position affects both the security discourse and the political development of the country. For Bülent Ecevit, who served four times as Prime Minister of Turkey between 1974 and 2002, 'Turkey's special geographical conditions require a special type of democracy' (cited in Aydinli and Waxman 2001: 385). Similarly, Turkey's geopolitics, according to the military bureaucracy, 'does not allow for more democracy' (cited in Bilgin 2005: 186). These views reflect the widespread understanding of the national security concept that focuses on Turkey's geopolitics in order to justify the state's attitude towards non-compliance with the rules of democracy (Bilgin 2005: 186).

In addition to references to Turkey's geographical position, fear of internal enemies is the most often quoted idea used to convince citizens of the wisdom of having a standing army to protect national security. The definition of 'national security' has changed over time in response to the country's political developments (Ustun and Senyuva 2013: 271), its scope being broadened in the 1990s. Internal threats, 'political Islam' and 'Kurdish separatism' were included in the concept of national security. This enlargement, first, strengthened the influence and the monopoly of the military over the definition of national security (Celenk 2009: 120–1). Second, it re-emphasised the army's self-image as guardian of the Republic. In 1997, for instance, the civilian government was accused of turning Turkey into an Islamic society and failing to deal with the terrorism threatening the existence of the state; it was therefore declared incompetent to resolve the on-going conflict with the Kurdistan Workers' Party (PKK). As a result, the TAF highlighted their vital role in maintaining the Republic (Demirel 2004: 130).

The military forces played an important role in establishing the Republic of Turkey and introducing reforms directed at westernising the country. Since then, the army has considered itself responsible for protecting such reforms and national security against potential threats (Aknur 2012: 203). In line with this duty, the military has determined such potential 'threats' to the nation's unity and adopted its policies accordingly (Turan 1997: 132). Creating an atmosphere of fear and having a narrow understanding of national security have a significant impact on individuals' liberties. The assumption that a 'coercive military response' is essential for the maintenance of security makes the use of arms an indispensable element of national security (Blanton 1999: 233–5). As a result, the concept of national security has become the government's most desirable tool for building a large standing army.

Civilian Input?

The interference of the military in politics limits the civilian contribution to the conceptualisation of national security policy. It poses a significant challenge for those who desire to question military-related issues in the public sphere. Yet, since national security is the main concern of the military, particularly until the 2000s, any civilian debate on the concept of national security has become taboo. Until 2002, national security was a 'taboo that everyone more or less knows about, yet which nobody dares to deal with because it is a "hear no evil, see no evil, and speak no evil" subject' (Narli 2009a: 64–5). Similarly, in a speech delivered at the Congress of the Motherland Party in 2001, Prime Minister Mesut Yilmaz defined 'national security' as a 'syndrome'. According to him, as noted by Bilgin (2005: 191), the national security syndrome prevented any democratic changes in Turkish domestic law, and the main problem, in addition to the broad definition of national security, was the fact that politicians and civilians are not included in the process of defining national security. In another speech at the meeting of the Motherland Party's Chairmanship Council, Yilmaz also maintained that '[National security] is an issue that concerns everyone in Turkey. Therefore it should be discussed not only by the political parties but by the public as well' (quoted in Bilgin 2005: 191).

Politicians' responses to this call for debate are important for demonstrating how they perceive national security. For instance, according to both the Turkish General Staff and the Minister of Defence,[2] 'although national security may indeed be an "issue that concerns everyone in Turkey", it need not be discussed in public'. This indicates that politicians were not ready to accept the necessity for opening a public debate on national security (Bilgin 2005: 192). It also illustrates that Turkey's political culture is not 'citizen-centred'. It is, rather, a reflection of a society in which issues labelled as 'national' are not subject to democratic debates and the control of parliament (Aydın 2009: 31).

The Exclusion of Women and Lesbian, Gay, Bisexual, Transgender, Queer and Intersex (LGBTQI) Individuals from the Standing Army

Since the TAF were seen as guardians of the modern new regime, the modernisation process has not been immune to militarism, which could not be maintained without appealing to gender roles. Women were expected to raise patriot children and become supporters of soldiers as wives and mothers during the construction of the nation-state discourse. Not only were they given the roles of educating the new generation to modernise and westernise the nation, but they were also expected to contribute to the war (Öztan 2018), even though they were excluded from the conscription system. Regarding the exclusion of women, when the law that considered military service compulsory in Turkey was introduced in 1927, a member of the Assembly raised the following question:

> if voting and becoming a candidate is a national issue, participating in the country's defence is also a similar duty. I realize that the first article of the compulsory military service law has only included men. I would like to ask whether you have taken women's services into consideration, or to what extent. (cited in Altınay 2004: 33).

The response to the question acknowledges that women contributed to the War of Independence by 'carrying ammunition, providing support services, or at times fighting with the enemy' (Altınay 2004: 49) and, in the future, if they were needed, women would contribute in the same way again without being subjected to conscription (Altınay 2004: 33). This response gave rise to another question: when do states need women in military roles?

One of the prominent examples of ways in which women were needed in the military occurred during Atatürk's modernisation process in the new Republic. The process created the figure of the new and modern woman. The story of Atatürk's adopted daughter, Sabiha Gökçen, who played an important role in the modernisation of women, exemplifies this well. During military operations in Dersim, a Kurdish-populated province, Gökçen wanted to join in as a combat pilot, given that she was trained as such. However, in order to be assigned the job, she, unlike her male colleagues, had to prove to Atatürk that her gender identity would not affect the nature of her work (Altınay 2004). Their conversation runs as follows:

> Atatürk: I will let you go ... if your desire to go is this strong. But this is a military operation and you can only join if the Commander in Chief, Marshall Çakmak, gives the appropriate permission. But you should not forget this: You are a girl. And the mission at hand is a very difficult one. You will be faced with a band of deceived men. They too have some weapons. In case of an accident, you might have to do emergency landing and surrender to them. You will not know what this means until it happens to you. Have you thought about what you would do in such a situation?
> Gökçen: You are right. The plane might always have a technical problem and force me to land, or it might crash. If something this unfortunate happens, don't you worry; I will never surrender to them alive. (quoted in Altınay 2004: 39)

This conversation suggests that women were seen as symbolic markers of the nation. Indeed, this was not specific to the case of Turkey. As a result of viewing women as the nation and the nation as women, protecting women and their honour became an additional motive for fighting wars (Peterson 1999). Therefore, any threat to women's bodies was perceived as a threat to the nation's honour. In the case of Gökçen, she still needed to be protected even though she was a soldier. Her willingness to fight and die in the face of any threat that might affect her honour – and by extension, the nation's honour – was a prerequisite for the job (Altınay

2004). This example also shows that the process of militarism affects both men and women's daily life, but in different ways, which are shaped by the assumptions attributed to the specific sexes (Enloe 2016).

There is a close relationship between militarism and gender inequality in that the exclusion of women may reduce their chances of reaching high rank (Golan 1997: 583–4). Also, not all men 'enjoy the privileges' of militarism. There is also a hierarchical chain amongst different types of masculinities: that is to say, not all masculinities enjoy the same 'privileges' or suffer the same 'pain' (Dowd et al. 2011: 210). R. W. Connell's hegemonic masculinities concept refers to this hierarchy and subordination among different kinds of masculinities. For Connell, the socially accepted masculine norms dominate and occupy a position at the top of the hierarchy: one that is promoted by institutions, such as militaries (Connell 2005: 77). In this context, given that the military is seen as a 'first step on the path to manhood' (Altinay 2009: 90), one needs to ask: what would happen if a man does not conform to the heterosexual norms of the military?

In Turkey, homosexuals are not subject to dismissal, but an individual who declares his homosexuality is allowed to claim exemption[3] under the 1927 Military Law No. 1111, Article 10(8), which regulates 'the principles relating to those who shall be subject to military service obligations and how these obligations shall be rendered'. The Article reads as follows: 'according to the Turkish Armed Forces Health Aptitude Regulations, those whose [level of] physical capability is not suitable for military service shall be exempted from military service'.[4] It is important to consider how homosexuals are exempted under this Article. Before the 2013 amendment of the Turkish Armed Forces Health Aptitude Regulations, Appendix-C Article 17(B)(3) considered 'homosexuality, transsexuality, transvestitism' as psychosexual diseases and stated that 'the psychosexual and sexual behavioural disorder must be visible in all aspects of the individual's life, and it must be established, through observation or documents, that this has or would create problems in a military environment'.[5]

In order to be declared unfit and, therefore, receive the 'rotten report (çürük raporu)', applicants must prove their homosexuality. This process might also include rectal examination, and evidence such as photographs or videos showing the applicant is passive (Biricik 2009: 113). As the Commission of European Communities' 2009 Progress Report stated,

> The Turkish armed forces have a health regulation which defines homosexuality as a 'psychosexual' illness and identifies homosexuals as unfit for military

service. Conscripts who declare their homosexuality have to provide photographic proof. A small number have had to undergo humiliating medical examinations.[6]

In 2013, the Article was amended and 17(B)(3) was abolished. As a result, homosexuality is no longer officially considered a disease. However, the amended Article now excludes people from military service based on their 'sexual identity and behavioural disorders'. LGBTQI individuals are now banned on the grounds that 'sexual manners and behaviour cause or are expected to cause problems of adaptation and functionality in a military environment'.[7]

The Institutionalisation of the Military's Political Role

As Samuel Huntington (1957: 85) states, 'in a democratic country the military may undermine civilian control and acquire great political power through the legitimate process and institutions of democratic government and politics'. Militaries may gain their extended power over social and political matters through both direct and indirect means. The Turkish case provides an excellent example of the indirect influence of the military on politics. The relationship between governments and the military, particularly since 1983, shows that the military has had indirect impacts on the domestic affairs of governments. Rather than using repressive methods and aiming at building a 'military government', the military has used legal and constitutional mechanisms, as well as cultural and historical pretexts, to maintain its privileged status in political matters. After each military intervention,[8] it provided itself with legal protections; it regarded itself as the guardian of the Republic instead of staying in power (Sakallioğlu 1997: 153), in this manner remaining present in civilian spheres. Consequently, the military has exerted an influence on institutions that are considered civil in democratic countries (Aydinli et al. 2006: 4). That is to say, since the creation of the Republic of Turkey in 1923, the TAF have occupied a dominant position because they are viewed as the guardian of the Republic. Therefore, the military has remained immune from parliamentary control and has had the power to control the political arena in Turkey (Cizre 2004: 113).

The creation of the National Security Council, as a 'legal mechanism to assure a voice for the military profession', and granting it the authority to consider security matters were the main pillars of the military's continuous influence on politics (Harris 1988: 182–3). Under the 1961 Constitution, the Council was created to 'communicate the requisite fundamental recommendations to the Council of Ministers with the purpose of assisting in the making of decisions related to national security and coordination'.[9] Then, Article 111 of the 1961 Constitution was amended as follows: 'the National Security Council recommends the necessary basic views for decisions to be taken in connection with national security and coordination'.[10] With this amendment, the Council was granted further privileges. For instance, it was authorised to adopt recommendations instead of expressing opinions (Sakallioğlu 1997: 157). The 1982 Constitution further reinforced the authority and duties of the Council. Under Article 118 of the 1982 Constitution,[11] the implementation of such recommendations was regarded as a priority (Sakallioğlu 1997: 157; Momayezi 1998: 11–12).

The 1982 Constitution, promulgated after the 1980 coup, is one of the military's vital tools. The new Constitution marked a different dimension in the political culture and restricted public participation in politics. Its provisions provided a legal basis to expand military power in governmental institutions (Sakallioğlu 1997: 162). Article 104 of the 1982 Constitution,[12] entitled 'duties and powers', granted the President the power to decide on a wide range of matters, including the declaration of a state of emergency. Similarly, under Article 108 of the 1982 Constitution,[13] the State Supervisory Council[14] must obtain the President's consent while investigating all public bodies. When we consider the fact that Kenan Evren, the soldier who led the 1980 coup, was President of the Republic between 1982 and 1989,[15] the rationale behind the extension of the President's power clearly pertained to the military's aim to control the political development of the government (Momayezi 1998: 11). Under Provisional Article 9, which stated that 'the President of the Republic may refer to the Turkish Grand National Assembly for further consideration on any Constitutional amendments adopted by the Assembly',[16] the President was authorised to veto such constitutional amendments. The Presidential Council also gained the power to review legislation on any subject, such as public order, martial law and national security. It appears that the 1982 Constitution reinforced the President's power and the competence of the National Security Council, and helped the military to maintain its status quo as guardian of the Republic (Momayezi 1998: 12–13).

The Impact of Conscription Systems on the Militarisation of Society

Historically, the objective of the army as an institution was initially limited to military affairs, but later it expanded to include social factors intertwined with everyday situations. Due to the disciplined and organised structure of the Armed Forces, the employment of conscripts in the civilian sphere became a conventional method used to respond to extraordinary situations, such as natural disasters, refugee 'crises' and other social problems threatening the unity and social welfare of states. Consequently, the distinction between civilian and military spheres became increasingly blurred and the military was fully integrated into social life (Mellors and McKean 1984: 33–4). In addition, compared to volunteer forces, the conscription system empowers states to reach males from diverse backgrounds and to influence wider segments of society. Being exposed to military values, either directly or indirectly, societies are more likely to show support for the Armed Forces. The reason is straightforward: familiarity breeds acceptance. It is not surprising, then, that increased interaction with these values and the military makes it difficult to challenge these well-established and familiar ideologies. Also, whoever rejects these values might be labelled either a 'coward' or a 'traitor'. Furthermore, social rewards for being loyal to these values and the legal and social mechanisms that are established to punish those who reject the system cause enormous difficulties for individuals (Choulis et al. 2019: 3–4). When citizens refuse to attend the military or comply with its laws, their social position becomes at risk due to the exalted status that conscription enjoys in societies (Burk 1995: 512). Objectors fight against exclusion and are treated as individuals unworthy of respect in democratic societies, and also continue to refuse conscription at the same time (Burk 1995: 511).

The conscription system shapes individuals' understanding of militarism and exposes them to more militaristic values. It should be noted that the conscription system also forms decision-makers' attitudes towards participating in war. Studies that examine the conscription systems during the nineteenth and twentieth centuries argue that countries with a history of war or those which experienced internal or external threats are more likely to adopt conscription systems (Asal et al. 2017: 1461). Research has also found a close relationship between the tendency to engage in military disputes and having a conscripted army. In other words, having a conscripted army increases the likelihood of waging wars (Poutvaara and Wagener 2007: 10). The conscription system and the fighting of wars are two phenomena that co-dependently feed each other. Parallel to these observations, in the early years of the Turkish Republic, the military's influence on young people's educational and ideological standpoints became visible in compulsory military service. Military training aimed not only at improving physical strength but also at 'modernising' youth by encouraging them to engage with the new Republic's objectives, such as the secularisation and westernisation of the country. Given the limited educational recourses and schools during this era, mainly in rural areas, the army became the school of the nation, and compulsory military service occupied a significant place in young people's lives (Jenkins 2007: 340–1). Further, militaries have social and cultural impacts on society, mostly linked with citizenship and nationhood. As a result, as 'repositories of mythical constructions of the past and embodiments of the nation's aspirations', militaries occupy dominant positions compared to other institutions (Krebs 2006: 17).

The TAF maintained their prominent position in the country and gained public consent using 'soft power' instead of creating a repressive military state. For example, the Armed Forces disseminated their ideology via military and non-military educational curriculums, maintained compulsory military service and used the media for such ends (Cizre 2004: 113–14).[17] The military also used informal tools, such as public speeches, to 'educate' the public about the security issues facing the country. Such tools effectively constructed a security culture (Narli 2009a: 58). The reason behind the military's strong presence in Turkey can, therefore, be explained by the dynamics of Turkish society. Militarist values, such as being a 'hero', being 'brave' and dying for an exalted duty – becoming a 'martyr', are embedded in the Turkish identity. Further, the importance attached to being a martyr makes mothers of soldiers proud of becoming mothers of martyrs. They believe that their sons died doing their exalted duty to protect the nation. It is customary at soldiers' funerals to hear statements such as 'martyrs never die, and the homeland will never be divided (şehitler ölmez vatan bölünmez)'. Mothers also beat drums at the funerals of their 'martyrs' to display their proud attitude. This is just another example of how militaristic values are integrated into society (Demirel 2004: 140).

To understand how such values become embedded in society, it is worth examining the way that Turkish textbooks emphasise the importance of serving in the army and becoming a soldier. The education system shapes society in a way that gives the military the legitimacy to intervene in the political arena. The importance of the military's presence in Turkish society is emphasised in school textbooks, daily conversations and social practices. School classes disseminate the idea that the Turkish military is 'the symbol of the unity of the Turkish nation and the guarantor of the nation's future' (Aknur 2012: 222–3). In secondary schools, National Security Classes (Milli Güvenlik Dersleri) are aimed at raising youth conscientiousness. The aim of the classes is explained in the *National Security Instruction Guide* (*Milli Savunma Öğretimi Yönetmeliği*):

> Enhancing, in accordance with the prerequisites of total war, the already present spirit and consciousness of national security in Turkish youth in order to protect the Turkish Independence and Republic with an ever increasing might and vigour under all conditions and against all violations.

The second aim is to introduce young people to

> the Armed Forces, to bind youth to the Armed Forces with love and affection, to ideologically prepare them for the basic knowledge of the main defence activities conducted by the Armed Forces; in this way, bringing them to a state where they can begin working in the Armed Forces or in active organs of civilian defence at any moment, creating a spirit of unity and cooperation, and thus cultivating a patriotic youth. (cited in Aydın 2009: 28)

In textbooks, the national security concept is addressed as 'a national cause, a matter of life and death that the state and the government and all citizens must undertake without hesitation with their hands on their hearts and minds'. Accordingly, students, exposed to such textbooks, 'will have acquired a sufficient degree of national security consciousness and culture and when service is required in national defence they shall blend this culture with the heroism which is present in our temperament and be worthy of our ancestors'. The idea of dying for the nation is disseminated among young people through statements such as 'we shall all work for this land, live for this land and die for this land'.[18] The most prominent sign of this aim can be seen in school celebrations and rituals. For example, until 2013, primary school students repeated every morning the national pledge of allegiance (*Andımız*): 'I am a Turk, I am honest, I am a hard worker, and my principle is to love the elderly, protect those younger than me and love my country more than myself. I offer my existence to the Turkish nation as a gift.'[19] By reading such textbooks and participating in these ceremonies, pupils are exposed to the view that military service has a vital importance in maintaining both the nation's spirit and its power because the military is portrayed as the only institution that instils such a spirit (Aydın 2009: 30).

The military's influence in Turkey is not only institutional but also cultural. In addition to the fear of losing its territorial integrity, Turkey's cultural and social features, which consider Turks as warriors and the military as the school of the nation, have constituted the main elements enabling the military to interfere in politics and blur the line between

civilian and military spheres. The belief that the military not only protects the nation against its enemies but also functions as the guardian of
democracy's fundamental principles has significant impacts on society's
perception of the military (Narli 2005: 157–8).

The Military's Decreasing Political Role in the
Justice and Development Party Era

The military has enjoyed a visible and dominant position in relation
to political matters. The importance of military service and trust in the
army are internalised in society. However, the army's intervention in
politics has been neutralised under the Justice and Development Party
(AKP). When the AKP came to power, Tayyip Erdoğan paved the way for
a gradual transformation of the military, instead of taking immediate
steps towards challenging the military's role in politics. Preparing society
for change was part of his agenda. To gain support, Erdoğan promised to
democratise the country and to join the EU. This necessitated a change in
the military's institutional structure and reforms were thus introduced to
fulfil EU requirements (Caliskan 2017: 98). Following the Copenhagen
criteria for becoming an EU member, Turkey has executed harmonisation reforms. These aim to reduce the institutional tools that enable the
military to interfere in politics (Narli 2009b: 434).

With the 2001 and 2004 constitutional amendments, several major
changes with enormous impacts on the military's institutional structure
were introduced. First, with the 7th EU harmonisation package, the role
of the National Security Council (NSC) was reduced to providing recommendations on national security.[20] Second, the NSC's influence on the
civilian sphere – namely, education, the media and art – was eliminated.
While the 6th EU harmonisation package had removed the members
of NSC from the High Audio-Visual Board, the 8th EU harmonisation
package removed the military representatives from the High Education
Board (Narli 2005: 164–7). Third, the 7th EU harmonisation package
amended the Military Criminal Code and abolished military trials of
civilians (Narli 2009b: 445–6). Further, in the 2010 referendum, the
majority supported amendments to the 1982 Constitution, which was
drafted by the military after the 1980 coup. One of these amendments
was the abolition of Article 15 of the Constitution, which granted military personnel immunity from prosecution. Thus, the two leaders of the
1980 coup, Kenan Evren and Tahsin Sarıkaya, were brought to trial. With
this amendment, the military no longer enjoys immunity and political
power; in fact, its public image was shaken (Keyman 2012).

These reforms not only transformed military power at the institutional level but also had an impact on society's perception of the military, thus inducing social change. The new political situation no longer considers the army's intervention in the political arena as a 'reliable' solution (Narli 2009b: 465). Indeed, Turkey has experienced an unprecedented cycle of events due to a failed coup attempt on 15 July 2016. Having followed Erdoğan's call to take to the streets,[21] people gathered to stand together against the attempted coup. While, on the one hand, soldiers confronted unarmed civilians, on the other hand civilian reaction to young conscripted soldiers was brutal. As a result, the military's image, which was socially accepted for so long, was destroyed. The soldier's body, which used to be considered as the nation's symbol, was damaged (Açıksöz 2017: 178). The conscripted soldier is seen as one step behind being a 'real man'. When he has completed his service, he can be considered ready to settle down. Although the soldier's uniformed body is masculinised, he is still a 'childishly innocent figure'. That is the reason why soldiers are mostly seen as *Mehmetçik* (Little Mehmet) and why, in the aftermath of the coup, the image of helpless young conscripts – the 'innocent *Mehmetçik*' – is considered morally disturbing (Açıksöz 2017: 178–9).

In the aftermath of the coup attempt, to maintain trust in the military and the motto of 'every Turk is born a soldier', officials categorised coupist soldiers as 'terrorists' to distinguish them from heroic soldiers. Those who died during the coup attempt were denied a funeral service, and a 'traitors' cemetery' was created for them (Açıksöz 2017: 179). Despite the battered image of the military, masculinity and militarism were valorised and, therefore, strengthened. The prevailing language in the democracy vigils glorified martyrdom and wounded warriors (Açıksöz 2017: 180). Those who opposed the coup acted in a militaristic way, reflecting the attitudes of a militarised society. While challenging the military, the urge to maintain militarist and gendered motives was kept alive. The irony runs as follows: challenging the military with militarist and masculine tools, chanting for the death penalty, and overemphasizing heroism and martyrdom. This is the irony that reproduces militarism in different ways.

Conclusion

Most of the people of the world who are militarized are not themselves in uniform. Most militarized people are civilians.

(Enloe 2016: 18)

The typical characteristics of civil–military relations in Turkey are society's acceptance of the military and its competence to protect the nation against all threats – international, domestic, political and so on (Aydinli 2009: 585). Military values are embedded in education, politics and everyday life, and any public debate about national security and any critique of the army can be seen as a threat in countries attaching significance to the army and to national defence. Similarly, any refusal of military service involves a range of difficulties. This is precisely the case because Turkey is ruled by a Constitution which is a product of the 1980 coup, and the idea that 'every Turk is born a soldier' still prevails (Çınar and Üsterci 2009b: 2). Yet, the military's sway over politics and its visible influence on nation-making not only impede any challenges to the army's dominant position but also demonstrate the pervasive militarist traditions in society (Demirel 2004: 139–40). These traditions deem the conscription system necessary for the state to defend its territories, while conscientious objection is viewed as a violation of responsibilities because military service is a duty for male citizens. Objectors are then perceived as 'lazy' and 'unwilling' to risk their lives, as opposed to others who join the army to protect the nation against a threat during war (Marcus 1997: 510). It would not, then, be unfair to claim that the conscription system contributes significantly to the militarisation of society by 'instilling . . . the view that killing for the home country is a patriotic duty' (Poutvaara and Wagener 2009: 17).

Notes

1. For instance, in Article 3(a) of the By-Law of Secretariat General of the National Security Council, 'national security' is defined as 'being able to resist all external or internal attacks, defeatist attempts, natural disasters and conflagrations. National security means to protect and maintain the state authority and using all national strength, efforts and activities for being victorious in a war.' Similarly, the General Assembly of the Lawsuit Department of the Council of the State defines 'national security' as the 'protect[ion] and secur[ity of] the legal entity of the State against the internal and external threats emerging throughout the country'. Furthermore, the 1983 Law number 2945 of the National Security Council and Secretariat General of the National Security Council defined 'national security' as 'the protection and maintenance of the constitutional order, national presence, integrity, all political, social, cultural and economic interests in international field as well as against any kind of internal and external threats, of the State (md.2/a)'. (These definitions are borrowed from Urhan and Çelik 2010: 11).
2. Bilgin (2005: 192) also gives Sabahattin Cakmakoglu's speech as an example, where he states: 'there is not any problem. National security policy does not

consist of personal assessments. It is developed by taking into consideration Turkey's strategic position and its neighbours.'

3. Historically, gay men were banned from military service. For instance, 'Don't Ask, Don't Tell' – the official US policy from 1993 to 2011 on homosexuals doing military service – banned gay people. Although this policy did not authorise the military to ask about a soldier's sexual orientation, disclosure of sexual identity resulted in dismissal from the military. The reason behind this implementation is that it would affect 'military performance' if known homosexuals were allowed to serve in the army (see Belkin 2003: 109). In Britain, the ban on homosexuals was lifted in 2000 following the ECtHR's decision that banning LGBTQI from military service is a violation of the right to privacy (see Belkin 2003: 110).

4. Law on Military Service Act No. 1111, 20 March 1927, Article 10(8).

5. Turkish Armed Forces Health Aptitude Regulations, Appendix-C Article 17 (B)(3).

6. Turkey 2009 progress report, Commission staff working document, SEC (2009) 1334 final, 14 October 2009, 26.

7. Turkish Armed Forces Health Aptitude Regulations, No. 86/11092, 8 October 1986, Appendix-C Amended Article 17(D)(4).

8. Since 1923, Turkey has experienced four military coups. (1) The Democrat Party came to power in 1950, but when economic conditions deteriorated and conflict between right and left wings arose, the military launched a coup on 27 May 1960 (Jenkins 2007: 341). (2) The military also intervened in politics on 12 March 1971 by giving a memorandum to Süleyman Demirel, the Prime Minister (Justice Party), which led to Demirel's resignation. (3) The military once again staged a coup due to the political unrest faced by the country in September 1980. This time, the military ruled the Republic for three years and issued the 1980 Constitution (Jenkins 2007: 342). (4) Finally, when the Islamist Welfare Party won the election in 1994 and became 'the largest party in parliament', Necmettin Erbakan's (the first Islamist Prime Minister) implementations were considered as a threat to secularism. This time, the military did not take power directly but instead issued a series of 'recommendations' (Jenkins 2007: 345).

9. 1961 Turkish Constitution No. 334, 9 July 1961, Article 111.

10. 1961 Turkish Constitution No. 334, 9 July 1961, amended Article 111.

11. Article 118 of the Constitution reads as follows: 'The National Security Council shall submit to the Council of Ministers its views on taking decisions and ensuring necessary coordination with regard to the formulation, establishment, and implementation of the national security policy of the State. *The Council of Ministers shall give priority consideration to the decisions of the National Security Council* concerning the measures that it deems necessary for the preservation of the existence and independence of the State, the integrity and indivisibility of the country, and the peace and security of society' (emphasis added).

12. According to Article 104, the President has the authority 'to proclaim martial law or a state of emergency, and to issue decrees having the force of law, by the decisions of the Council of Ministers under his/her chairpersonship, to submit

to referendum, if he/she deems it necessary, laws regarding amendment to the Constitution, to decide on the use of the Turkish Armed Forces'.

13. According to Article 108, 'the State Supervisory Council which shall be attached to the Office of the Presidency of the Republic, with the purpose of ensuring the lawfulness, regular and efficient functioning and improvement of administration, conduct all inquiries, investigations and inspections of all public bodies and organizations, all enterprises in which those public bodies and organizations share more than half of the capital, public professional organizations, employers' associations and labour unions at all levels, and public welfare associations and foundations, upon the request of the President of the Republic'.

14. 'The main function of the council is to audit governance in terms of compliance with legal regulations, in coordination with high efficiency. The council is under the direct authority of the President of the Republic of Turkey.' Available at: <https://en.wikipedia.org/wiki/State_Supervisory_Council> (last accessed 24 August 2017).

15. Kenan Evren was elected as President of the Republic under Provisional Article 1 of the 1982 Constitution Provisional, which stated that 'on the proclamation, under lawful procedure, of the adoption by referendum of the Constitution as the Constitution of the Republic of Turkey, the Chairman of the Council of National Security and Head of State at the time of the referendum, shall assume the title of President of the Republic and shall exercise the Constitutional functions and powers of the President of the Republic for a period of seven years'.

16. Provisional Article 9 of the 1982 Constitution.

17. Military schools were shut down after the 15 July coup attempt in 2016.

18. All these aims and definitions are cited in Aydın (2009: 28–9).

19. The oath is available at: <https://en.wikipedia.org/wiki/Student_Oath_(Turkey)> (last accessed 28 January 2021).

20. 'The NSC is to determine national security concept and develop ideas about the security in accordance with the state's security approach and recommend these security views to the Council of Ministers' (Narli 2005: 164).

21. 'Thousands went out to the streets with the authority of the government to stop the coup and protect the nation against the putschists who have become its abject. In the aftermath of the failed coup attempt, streets and squares, formerly banned for dissident protestors, were filled with people celebrating the "glorious defense of democracy," waving Turkish flags, chanting slogans against the coup, and shouting, "Allahu Ekber." The call to be on the streets during and after the coup attempt ostensibly was for unity' (Başdaş 2017: 186).

CHAPTER 2

Conscientious Objection and International Law

Introduction

Conscientious objectors' personal and moral convictions compel them to disobey the legal obligations that contradict their conscience. Once they have decided that the duty to obey clashes with their moral convictions, they commit the act of civil disobedience. When the law forces people to act against their conscience, such as compelling pacifists to join the military, it is hard to assess the moral convictions that people use to justify their acts of civil disobedience. This is the reason why responses to such a conflict between conscience and law are not well established (Greenawalt 1991: 174). Recent developments show an increased tendency towards recognising the right to conscientious objection at an international level. Yet, conscientious objectors are still exposed to human rights violations, such as discrimination and imprisonment, because of their objection. Some states still ignore the fact that all individuals should be entitled to take responsibility for their own beliefs and not be forced to act against their convictions (Major 2001: 2). As indicated by Matthew Lippman (1990: 65), 'conscientious objection is a blatant omission from the list of internationally mandated human rights'. Similarly, at the regional level, while the (refined) jurisprudence of the ECtHR indicates that the right to freedom of religion, thought and conscience covers the right to conscientious objection, its implementation differs from one state to another. Conscientious objection is considered as a conflict between states' interest in securing their territories and their citizens' right to religion, thought and conscience (Gilbert 2001: 1). In other words, conscientious objectors challenge the duty to protect the homeland against all kinds of threats. As a result, the issue of granting the right to conscientious objection remains controversial (Moskos and

Chambers 1993c: 3). Since the implementation of the right to conscientious objection may vary depending on how states interpret human rights, determination of the scope of such a right involves some difficulties. The question of whether all beliefs constitute a legitimate ground for refusing military service remains unanswered (Hammer 2001: 207–8). As indicated by Jeroen Temperman (2010: 211), fair and equal recognition of the right to conscientious objection is not an easy task, requiring multiple human rights issues to be considered.

Given this background, this chapter focuses on the conflict between conscience and law, which raises controversial questions over the responsibility of states in accommodating different forms of moral beliefs. It aims to answer the question of whether the right to religion, conscience and thought constitutes a legal ground for claiming the right to conscientious objection. In this context, it examines the right to religion, conscience and thought in the light of the ECHR and the case law of the ECtHR. Although the chapter adopts the right to freedom of thought, conscience and religion as a main legal ground for recognition of the right to conscientious objection to study the obstacles faced by objectors, it also examines conscientious objection in the light of Article 14 of the ECHR (protection from discrimination). It analyses the unequal treatment received by conscientious objectors with criminal records. Therefore, it aims to answer the question of whether failing to distinguish conscientious objectors from other law-breakers violates Article 14 of the ECHR. Finally, it analyses the right to conscientious objection under the International Covenant on Civil and Political Rights (ICCPR) and the case law of Human Rights Committee.

The Right to Conscientious Objection in the European Human Rights System

The Right to Conscientious Objection and Article 9 of the ECHR

Although the relevant international instruments do not explicitly recognise the right to conscientious objection in international society, the right to freedom of thought, conscience and religion is commonly interpreted as encompassing the right to conscientious objection. Conscientious objection derives from 'principles and reasons of conscience, including profound convictions, arising from religious, moral, ethical, humanitarian or other motives'.[1] Many recommendations of the Council of Europe also recognise freedom of thought and conscience, and demonstrate that the right to conscientious objection derives from this basic human right. Recommendation No. R (87) 8 of the Committee of Ministers of the

Council of Europe states that 'anyone liable to conscription for military service who, for compelling reasons of conscience, refuses to be involved in the use of arms, shall have the right to be released from the obligation to perform such service'.[2] Similarly, Recommendation 1518 of the Council of Europe Parliamentary Assembly notes that 'the right of conscientious objection is a fundamental aspect of the right to freedom of thought, conscience and religion enshrined in the Universal Declaration of Human Rights and the European Convention on Human Rights'.[3] In view of these definitions, one needs to ask whether Article 9 of the ECHR can be considered as a legitimate ground for conscientious objection and then investigate the application of Article 9 of the Convention to cases that emerged from the conflict between individuals' deepest convictions and the law that obliges them to act against those convictions.

Article 9 of the Convention guarantees the right to freedom of thought, conscience and religion. It reads as follows:

1. Everyone has the right to freedom of thought, conscience and religion; this right includes freedom to change his[her] religion or belief and freedom, either alone or in community with others and in public or private, to manifest his religion or belief, in worship, teaching, practice and observance.
2. Freedom to manifest one's religion or beliefs shall be subject only to such limitations as are prescribed by law and are necessary in a democratic society in the interests of public safety, for the protection of public order, health or morals, or for the protection of the rights and freedoms of others.[4]

The freedom to comply with the requirements of religion invites a few worries. The first concern pertains to the sincerity of individuals who want to obtain exemption from a legal responsibility based on their religious belief, which prohibits fulfilling such legal responsibilities. That is to say, exemption claims grounded on religious beliefs require a balance between individuals' right not be 'compelled to act contrary to their deepest convictions' and the state's interest in testing the sincerity of conscientious objection in order to distinguish between genuine acts and others intended to avoid legal responsibilities (Leigh and Born 2008: 75). Regarding such a concern, the ECtHR held that Article 9 of the Convention 'denotes views that attain a certain level of cogency, seriousness, cohesion and importance'.[5] Therefore, to ensure protection under Article 9, any claimed belief must meet a minimum threshold. However, the question of how the authorities could measure the sincerity of conscientious objectors remains challenging.[6] The second concern is related to defining religion. Many religions include responsibilities

and some kinds of prohibition, which might put believers into conflict with legal obligations that contradict the believer's inner convictions. In this sense, defining religion also means determining the legal
framework of exemptions, yet international courts refrain from defining
religion. As a result, conflicts between legal obligations and religious
prohibitions 'become more frequent' (Ahdar and Leigh 2005: 125).

The protection of Article 9 of the Convention covers religious beliefs –
not only long-established ones but also new forms of belief – and a wide
range of philosophical convictions. Therefore, protecting a broad range of
beliefs inevitably requires a flexible and workable definition of religion
(Harris et al. 2009: 426–7). Such a definition determines which legal regulations are applicable to cases demanding exemption from military service. In other words, given that individuals assign a different meaning to
religion, defining religion in legal terms becomes essential for regulating
which of these meanings are entitled to protection. In a nutshell, to recognise individuals' right based on their religions, one must clarify what constitutes a religion (Ahdar and Leigh 2005: 111). It is important to consider
that the main aim of defining religion is to clarify its function in obtaining
an exemption from legal responsibilities (for example, from military service) or a legal benefit (such as charitable status) (Ahdar and Leigh 2005:
114). For the purposes of this chapter, the legal significance of the religion
will be examined in the context of exemption from military service.

The definition of religion cannot be found in international documents but attempts have been made by domestic courts to establish one
(Lerner 2006: 6). For this reason, although the main focus of this chapter
is on the ECtHR's case law, it is helpful to examine how domestic courts
define religion. For instance, the High Court of Australia focuses on the
legal consequences of religion and adopts the view that

> the relevant inquiry is to ascertain what is meant by religion as an area of
> legal freedom or immunity and that inquiry looks to those essential indicia
> of religion which attract that freedom or immunity. It is in truth an inquiry
> into legal policy. (cited in Ahdar and Leigh 2005: 114)

Religion for the US Supreme Court also

> has reference to one's views of [their] relations to [their] Creator, and to the
> obligations they impose of reverence for [their] beings and character, and
> of obedience to his will. It is often confounded with the cultus or form of
> worship of a particular sect, but is distinguishable from the latter. (cited in
> Lerner 2006: 6)

According to the Canadian Supreme Court in *R v. Big M Drug Mart Ltd*,

> the essence of the concept of freedom of religion is the right to entertain such religious beliefs as a person chooses, the right to declare religious beliefs openly and without fear of hindrance or reprisal, and the right to manifest belief by worship and practice or by teaching and dissemination. But the concept means more than that. Freedom can primarily be characterized by the absence of coercion or constraint. If a person is compelled by the state or the will of another to a course of action or inaction, which he would not otherwise have chosen, he is not acting of his own volition and he cannot be said to be truly free. (cited in Ahdar and Leigh 2005: 99)

This passage, which clarifies what freedom of religion is, illustrates the impacts of coercion on the essence of freedom. Applying this definition to a conscientious objection case shows that compulsory military service is a clear example of the state's coercion of individuals whose conscience requires them not to join the army and take up arms. In this sense, having the freedom not to be compelled to take up arms, the right to conscientious objection has an important role in preserving personal convictions. However, forcing people to complete military service prohibits individuals from acting according to their conscience or religion and obligates them to *act* against their beliefs. Therefore, the right to conscientious objection serves a very important purpose: assigning the right to behave in accordance with one's religious dictates (Wolff 1982: 68).

Forum Internum

Although the formulation of Article 9 of the Convention seems clear, it requires a distinction to be drawn between the passive aspects of the right to freedom of thought, conscience and religion and the active aspects of the right to manifest religion or belief. The Article provides both the right to freedom of thought, conscience and religion, which constitutes the internal aspects of the right, and the right 'to manifest a religion or belief in worship, teaching, practice and observance', which constitutes the external aspects of the right (Cumper 2001: 313). It is worth clarifying that the right's active aspects do not necessarily require the performance of a positive act. It also includes the rejection of performing a positive act. In the case of refusing to take an active part in the army, even though individuals refuse to participate in military service, this objection is still an expression or a manifestation of a particular religion or belief (Evans 2008b: 284).

Article 9(1) recognises that everyone has the right to freedom of thought, conscience and religion. However, the Article is applied in a very restricted manner that considers this right to relate merely to *forum internum*, the individual's inner belief (Evans 2008a: 292). In the international arena, the internal aspects of the right to freedom of conscience are protected with no derogation or limitation (Hammer 2001: 71–2). Problems arise when individuals *behave* in accordance with their conscience, asserting the external aspects of the right to conscience (Evans 2008a: 292). Such a narrow interpretation of the right to *forum internum* is misleading. While they appear to affect merely *forum externum*, state actions intended to repress a particular belief could affect the *forum internum*. Despite this, until the dissenting opinion in the case of *Eweida and Others v. the UK*,[7] judicial bodies avoided considering how limitations on the manifestation of conscience affect the *forum internum* (Hammer 2001: 73).[8]

Forum internum has been granted repeated recognition by the Strasbourg organs, which consider the *forum internum* as an inviolable part of the right to thought, conscience and religion. Therefore, it does not allow any limitations. Yet such recognition in practice is not put into effect. Until the dissenting opinion of *Eweida and Others v. the UK*, while dealing with individuals' complaints, European institutions have not considered the limitations on *forum externum*, requiring individuals to act against their beliefs, as a violation of *forum internum*. Rather, these cases are examined under other articles, such as the prohibition of discrimination (Taylor 2005: 119).

In joint partly dissenting opinion, Judges Vucinic and De Gaetano highlighted the impacts of limitations on *forum externum* on *forum internum*. The judges stated that

> we are of the view that once that a *genuine* and *serious* case of conscientious objection is established, the State is obliged to respect the individual's freedom of conscience both positively (by taking reasonable and appropriate measures to protect the rights of the conscientious objector) and negatively (by refraining from actions which punish the objector or discriminate against him or her).[9]

The judges also suggested that

> no one should be forced to act against one's conscience or be penalized for refusing to act against one's conscience. Although freedom of religion and freedom of conscience are dealt with under the same Article of the

Convention, there is a fundamental difference between the two [. . .] Even Article 9 hints at this fundamental difference: whereas the word 'conscience' features in 9 § 1, it is conspicuously absent in 9 § 2. Conscience – by which is meant moral conscience – is what enjoins a person at the appropriate moment to do good and to avoid evil. In essence, it is a judgment of reason whereby a physical person recognizes the moral quality of a concrete act that he is going to perform, is in the process of performing, or has already completed. This rational judgment on what is good and what is evil, although it may be nurtured by religious beliefs, is not necessarily so, and people with no particular religious beliefs or affiliations make such judgments constantly in their daily lives.[10]

This passage shows that the dissenting judges attached great importance to conscience in this specific case rather than religion. Furthermore, by pointing out the 'conspicuous absence' of conscience from the scope of Article 9(2), the judges considered conscience as an absolute right, which cannot be exposed to the limitations of Article 9(2) (Leigh and Hambler 2014: 7). To elaborate, as indicated by Carolyn Evans, when individuals are forced to act against their conscience because they fear being penalised for their refusal, this has an impact on *forum internum* (Evans 2003: 76). As pointed out by Paul Taylor (2005: 116–17), Evans suggests *forum internum* should be interpreted inclusively. In a review of European cases[11] concerning the legal obligations requiring individuals to act against their beliefs, Evans states that:

in neither case did the action of the State go so far that it made it impossible (or even particularly difficult) for the individuals to maintain their internal beliefs, but in each case the State required the individuals to act in a way that they felt was in direct contradiction to the requirements of those beliefs. They were in effect being asked to recant, by their behaviour, their religion. This conflict between the behaviour required of them and their beliefs was such that it arguably interfered with the internal as well as the external realm. (cited in Taylor 2005: 116–17)

Furthermore, Andrew Ahdar and Ian Leigh (2005: 125–6) draw attention to the fact that limitations on the manifestation of belief – external aspects of belief – might create a misperception that individuals are free to choose what they want to believe yet cannot act accordingly. Therefore, these limitations on external freedom, which do not allow people to 'accompany their belief by deeds', might have undermining effects on internal freedom as well.

Forum Externum

The wording of Article 9(1) raises many concerns because it states that 'this right includes [. . .] the right to manifest [their] religion or belief, in worship, teaching, practice and observance'.[12] There is no reference to the manifestation of conscience in the Article; it provides only the right to manifest religion and beliefs. As Malcom Evans (2001: 214) asks, 'does the use of term "belief" extend the freedom of manifestation beyond the scope of religion and apply it to other patterns of "thought and con-science" referred to in the opening affirmation of the right?' In other words, the questions that have to be considered here are: is there a right to manifest non-religious beliefs? When do conscientious objectors need to follow their conscience? Do they still have the right to manifest it? The wording of Article 9 makes it difficult to provide a straightforward answer.

The difference between the wording of Article 9(1) and that of Arti-cle 9(2) raises the subject of whether this means that the manifestation of the right to conscience and thought is excluded from the ambit of Article 9. This has been a matter of dispute amongst scholars. The dif-ference in the wording of Article 9 of the Convention leaves room to argue that the Article excludes manifestation of thought and conscience from the scope of the protection (Taylor 2005: 204). According to this view, Article 9 of the Convention protects not only the right to thought, conscience and religion but also the right to manifest religion or belief. However, other expressions of thought and conscience, which do not constitute a manifestation in the context of Article 9 of the Convention, are protected under Article 10 of the Convention (Evans 2008b: 284–5). That is, the term 'manifestation', used in and protected under Article 9 of the Convention, encompasses expressions related solely to religion or belief (Cumper 2001: 320). Malcom Evans also reserves the term 'manifestation' for the right to religion. Accordingly, religious beliefs can be expressed and manifested, but thought and conscience can only be expressed and are protected under Article 10. Therefore, Article 9(2) is not applicable.

Contrary to this position, Peter Edge (1996: 43) argues that it is hard to claim that excluding thought and conscience from the qualifying Article 9(2) is important. For him, 'these separate terms are indicative, rather than definitive, of some element common to all the beliefs protected by the Article 9'. Furthermore, Article 9 of the ECHR is based on Article 18 of the Universal Declaration of Human Rights (UDHR).[13] The main reason for relying on the UDHR was to be consistent with the definitions and principles of UN human rights law. In the UDHR, the terms 'thought' and 'conscience' were used with religion to include non-religious beliefs within the scope of protection as well. In that sense, freedom of thought and conscience and freedom of religion complement each other and, therefore, deserve the same protection. The omission of thought and conscience from Article 9(2) of the Convention does not mean the exclusion of thought and conscience from the protection of Article 9(2) (Taylor 2005: 205–6). Yet, it is important to consider the fact that although the distinction between Article 9(1) and Article 9(2) should not be interpreted in a way that limits the effectiveness of the Convention, excluding manifestation of conscience from the scope of the Article raises some difficulties, particularly about what the term belief covers – what kind of belief gives rise to the manifestation of a right under the Convention (Evans 2008b: 286). In this regard, the next question that has to be considered here is: what form of belief gives rise to the right to freedom of manifestation under Article 9 of the Convention?

What is Considered 'Practice'?

The right to conscientious objection, which leads to a conflict between states and individuals, has been widely recognised. Yet, the scope of the right remains controversial. Given the lack of consistent case laws on the scope of the right to conscientious objection, it becomes essential to clarify what kind of belief actually falls within the scope of the right to freedom of religion (Gilbert 2001: 1). This requires an investigation into whether refusing military service constitutes practising as a protected form of manifestation of belief under Article 9(1) of the Convention, which recognises the manifestation of religion or belief in the form of 'practice, worship, teaching, or observance'.

Even though there is a wide range of activities that might be considered as practice, in the case of *Arrowsmith v. the UK*, the European Commission dealt with the issue in a manner that excludes a range of eligible manifestations (Taylor 2005: 210). In this case, the applicant, as a pacifist, was convicted because of the leaflets she distributed to troops – leaflets that urged soldiers not to serve in Northern Ireland. She alleged that her conviction violated her right to manifest her pacifist belief under Article 9 of the Convention.[14] Whether pacifism was a belief and whether distributing pacifist leaflets was a manifestation as guaranteed in Article 9(2) of the Convention were the issues that had to be dealt with (Evans 2008b: 289). For the first issue, the Commission accepted that pacifism is protected under Article 9 of the Convention:

> the Commission is of the opinion that pacifism as a philosophy [. . .] falls within the ambit of the right to freedom of thought and conscience. The

attitude of pacifism may therefore be seen as a belief ('conviction') protected by Article 9(1). It remains to be determined whether or not the distribution by the applicant of the leaflets here in question was also protected by Article 9(1) as being the manifestation of her pacifist beliefs.[15]

For the second issue, the Commission stated that

the term 'practice' as employed in Article 9(1) does not cover each act which is *motivated or influenced* by a religion or a belief.

When individuals' actions do not actually express the belief concerned they cannot be considered to be as such protected by Article 9(1), even when they are motivated or influenced by it.[16] (emphasis added)

In *Arrowsmith v. United Kingdom*, the Commission applied definitional balancing to limit the scope of protection provided by Article 9. It rejected claims because they were not based on practices deemed to be mandatory by religion (Leigh and Hambler 2014: 10). Although the Commission certainly indicates that an act that is motivated by religion or belief does not constitute practice, it does not clarify which acts are to be considered a practice to gain protection under Article 9 of the Convention (Evans 2003: 113). Thus, *Arrowsmith* does not give a clear understanding of the acts covered by the term 'practice'. Furthermore, actions that are merely influenced by religion or belief are excluded from the scope of the protection provided by Article 9. In this regard, for an act to be considered as a practice under Article 9, it requires a direct link between belief and actions (Evans 2003: 115).

For an act to be regarded as a manifestation of belief, the Arrowsmith test requires actions to be religiously compelled rather than religiously motivated. However, this distinction demands that courts investigate which acts are requirements of the applicants' belief. If the court interprets the requirements of applicants' beliefs differently, applicants might be found insincere or lacking a proper understanding of their belief (Ahdar and Leigh 2005: 164). Furthermore, in order to gain protection under Article 9(2), applicants are forced to prove that their action 'is mandated by the religion or belief system espoused' (Leigh and Hambler 2014: 10). However, there is inadequate evidence to conclude that the text of Article 9 limits the manifestations of religion merely to acts considered as duties (Ahdar and Leigh 2005: 165). The requirement of being compelled to act in a specific way rather than being motivated limits the applicability of Article 9. It restricts freedom of religion in the definitional stage. Claims regarding religious rights are rejected without even assessing if the interference is 'necessary in a democratic society', as provided in Article 9(2) of the Convention (Leigh 2012: 243).

While the Court's approach in the Arrowsmith case might prevent 'bogus or trivial beliefs' from being granted legal exemptions, it also empowers domestic courts to determine whether a practice is mandated by religion (Harris et al. 2009: 433). Similarly, in the *Valsamis v. Greece* case,[17] the applicant's daughter 'was asked to take part in the celebration of the National Day'.[18] The applicant asserted that 'pacifism is a fundamental tenet of their religion and forbids any conduct or practice associated with war or violence, even indirectly'.[19] Although she informed the school administration that 'her religious beliefs forbade her joining in the commemoration of a war',[20] she was suspended from school because she failed to attend the celebration.[21] The applicant emphasised that Article 9 'guaranteed her right to the negative freedom not to manifest, by gestures of support, any convictions or opinions contrary to her own'.[22] However, the Court concluded[23] that 'the obligation to take part in the school parade was not such as to offend her parents' religious convictions'.[24] In this case, the Court refused the claims due to its 'own assessment' of the parade as a celebration of peace rather than war (Ahdar and Leigh 2005: 164). The Court made a 'dangerous mistake' because it 'in effect substituted its judgment for the conscience of the person involved, defining what was "reasonable" for them to believe' (Harris et al. 2009: 433).

Regarding the *Arrowsmith v. United Kingdom* case, it is evident that the Strasbourg organs, when dealing with the issue of what counts as religion or belief, adopted a broad approach. But, when deciding if the act counts as a manifestation, they adopt a limited approach (Evans 2008a: 295). However, Mr Opsahl, in his dissenting opinion, refused to adopt this approach. For him,

> an act cannot be interfered with merely because it has been declared unlawful [. . .] Art. 9 must, in principle, be applicable to a great many acts which are not, on their face, necessarily manifesting the underlying or motivating belief, if that is what they genuinely do.[25]

In line with this dissenting opinion, the Court also took a more inclusive approach in *Eweida and Ors v. the United Kingdom*.[26] In the present case, the applicants – those not permitted to wear a cross at the workplace and those expected either to register as same-sex couples or to accept counselling – alleged that they had suffered religious discrimination at work; the government, however, based its arguments on the case law of the Court and argued that 'behaviour which was motivated or inspired by religion or belief, but which was not an act of practice of a religion in a generally recognized form, fell outside the protection of Article 9'.[27] According to the Court,

> in order to count as a 'manifestation' within the meaning of Article 9, the act in question must be intimately linked to the religion or belief. An example would be an act of worship or devotion which forms part of the practice of a religion or belief in a generally recognized form. However, the manifestation of religion or belief is not limited to such acts; the existence of a sufficiently close and direct nexus between the act and the underlying belief must be determined on the facts of each case. In particular, there is no requirement on the applicant to establish that he or she acted in fulfilment of a duty mandated by the religion in question.[28]

Furthermore, in the joint partly dissenting opinion of Judges Bratza and David Thór Björgvinsson in *Eweida and Others v. the UK*, it is stated that

> the 'manifestation' of religion or belief within the meaning of Article 9 is not limited to acts of worship or devotion which form part of the practice of a religion or belief 'in a generally recognized form'. Provided a sufficiently close and direct nexus between the act and the underlying belief exists, there is no obligation on an applicant to establish that he or she acted in fulfilment of a duty mandated by the religion.[29]

In the present case, the Court weakened the impact of the definitional balancing approach on limiting the effectiveness of Article 9. Therefore, in *Eweida and Others v. the United Kingdom*, the Court interpreted the definitional approach clearly and explicitly. The necessity test, which requires individuals to prove that their act is mandated by religion or belief to gain protection as guaranteed in Article 9 of the Convention, was overruled. Furthermore, by requiring 'a sufficiently close and direct nexus between the act and the underlying belief', the Court clarified that the main requirement to gain protection under Article 9 is that the belief is 'cogent and important' (Leigh and Hambler 2014: 11).

In the same vein, in its judgement on the *Jakopski v. Poland* case, the Court did not apply the definitional filter. Instead, it adopted a broad interpretation of Article 9 of the Convention (Leigh and Hambler 2014: 10). In the present case, the applicant, a prisoner, informed the prison authorities about his religious precepts and requested a meat-free diet.[30] However, his request was refused on the grounds that preparing 'vegetarian meals in prison would have put too much strain on the authorities'.[31] The applicant asserted that refusing his religious precepts and meat-free diet requirements breached his right to manifest his religion.[32] The Court recalled its *Cha'are shalom ve tsedek* judgement, in which it held that 'observing dietary rules can be considered a direct expression of beliefs in practice in the sense of Article 9',[33] then concluded that 'the applicant's decision to adhere to a vegetarian diet can be regarded as motivated or inspired by a religion and was not unreasonable'.[34] Therefore, 'the refusal to provide him with meat-free meals amounted to an interference with his rights guaranteed by Article 9 of the Convention'.[35] Furthermore, in the case of *Bayatyan v. Armenia*, while assessing whether conscientious objection falls within the ambit of Article 9, the Court focused on motivations which are based on sincerely held beliefs, rather than investigating whether the act was the requirement of such a belief (Leigh and Hambler 2014: 10–11).

In sum, the manifestation of religion or belief is recognised in the form of practice, worship, teaching or observance in Article 9 of the ECHR. Although the wording of the Article refers to manifestation in relation to worship and observance, and limits manifestation to religion or belief, the manifestation of conscientious belief can be considered as a form of practice and, as such, gains protection under both articles (Hammer 2001: 121). To gain protection under Article 9, one does not necessarily have to believe in a 'supreme being'. European jurisprudence makes it clear that the protection of Article 9 of the Convention is not limited to religious beliefs: it includes all forms of belief, including atheism and agnosticism (Edge 1996: 42). Article 9 also protects a wide range of philosophical beliefs, as long as they 'attain a certain level of cogency, seriousness, cohesion and importance'.[36] As a result, one can claim that refusing to complete military service is recognised as a manifestation of belief. Although conscientious objection raises controversial issues under the international instruments and case law, pacifism has been acknowledged as a valid and secular belief. It is a legitimate ground for asserting the right to conscientious objection (Hammer 2001: 123–4).

Case Law of the European Commission and ECtHR and Conscientious Objection

Traditional Approach to Conscientious Objection

Historically, the European Commission ruled that international law does not recognise the right to conscientious objection. It concluded in particular, in numerous cases, that there is no right to conscientious objection. The Commission preferred to examine the cases involving religious claims under other relevant articles instead of Article 9 of the Convention. Consequently, the jurisprudence of the Commission regarding Article 9 has been underdeveloped. It has been suggested that avoidance of applying Article 9 to religious claims resulted in 'slow development of the right to conscientious objection' (Harris et al. 2009: 432–3). For a long period, the Commission's focus remained solely on the wording of Article 9 of the Convention, which makes no explicit reference to the right to conscientious objection. In several cases, the Commission claimed that the only reference to conscientious objection can be found in Article 4(3)(b), which excludes 'any service of a military character or, in case of conscientious objectors in countries where they are recognized, service exacted instead of compulsory military service' from the scope of forced labour. The Commission referred to forced labour when evaluating conscientious objection claims despite it having no connection with the right to thought, conscience and religion. Considering Article 4, the Commission concluded that the recognition of alternative service is only an option, not an obligation. During this period, applications requesting recognition as conscientious objectors were confronted with this distorted interpretation of Article 4(3)(b) and, as such, were deprived of any protection under Article 9 (Muzny 2012: 137). Some analysis of these cases will be helpful for understanding the shift from a traditional interpretation of the right to freedom of thought, conscience and religion to a growing recognition of the right to conscientious objection in international law.

When a Jehovah's Witness refused to comply with military orders following his beliefs in the *Grandrath v. Germany* case,[37] the Commission did not consider the issue under Article 9 but Article 4(3)(b). The applicant alleged that the criminal proceedings launched against him – because he refused to perform military service – interfered with his right to freedom of conscience and religion under Article 9 of the ECHR.[38] However, according to the Commission,

> while Article 9 guarantees the right to freedom of thought, conscience and religion in general, Article 4 of the Convention contains a provision which expressly deals with the question of compulsory service exacted in the place of military service in the case of conscientious objectors.[39]

Although the applicant alleged a violation of Article 9 of the Convention, the Commission did not consider the case under Article 9 and observed that, as 'it is expressly recognized that civilian service may be imposed on conscientious objectors as a substitute for military service, it must be concluded that objections of conscience do not, under the Convention, entitle a person to exemption from such service'.[40]

Similarly, in the case of *Bayatyan v. Armenia*,[41] the applicant alleged that 'his conviction for refusal to serve in the army had unlawfully interfered with his right to freedom of thought, conscience and religion'.[42] The Court considered the claims in the context of Article 4(3) instead of Article 9 of the ECHR. The Court referred to the existing case law regarding the right to the conscientious objection claims.[43] It first referred to *X v. Austria*,[44] in which the Commission considered Article 4(3)(b) of the Convention while dealing with the disputed matter. According to the Commission, the terms, 'in countries where they are recognized' in Article 4(3)(b), give the High Contracting Parties a choice to recognise the right to conscientious objection. Thus, Article 9 of the Convention was qualified by Article 4(3)(b) and did not obligate states to recognise the right to conscientious objection.[45] Furthermore, in the case of *Ulke v. Turkey*, the Court reminded us that the 'applicant's multiple consecutive convictions for his repeated refusals to wear military uniform on the grounds of conscience' were not examined under Article 9 of the Convention.[46] Instead, the Court based its decision on Article 3 of the Convention and concluded that 'these multiple convictions were considered to amount to degrading treatment as they caused the applicant severe pain and suffering which went beyond the normal element of humiliation inherent in any criminal sentence or detention'.[47] Having referred to the arguments raised in the *Ulke v. Turkey* case (see below), the Court concluded in *Bayatyan v. Armenia* that 'Article 9 does not guarantee the right to conscientious objection'.[48]

In *Ulke v. Turkey*,[49] the applicant, as a pacifist and a conscientious objector, alleged that 'he had been prosecuted and convicted on account of his beliefs'.[50,51] Although the applicant relied on Articles 3 and 9,[52] the Court did not examine the case within the framework of Article 9 of the Convention. The Court relied on Article 3 of the ECHR, which states that 'no one shall be subjected to torture or to inhuman or degrading treatment or punishment', while concluding that convictions on the grounds of refusing to wear military uniform were a kind of humiliation.[53] The Court called attention to the risk of repeated imprisonment and, therefore, highlighted how the applicant

> has already been sentenced eight times to terms of imprisonment for refusing to wear uniform. Upon each release from prison after serving his sentence, he has been escorted back to his regiment, where, upon his refusal to perform military service or put on uniform, he has once again been convicted and transferred to prison.[54]

The Court was also aware of the lack of provisions in Turkish law and stipulated that, 'because of general legislation, applicant ran and still runs the risk of an interminable series of prosecutions and criminal convictions'.[55] The whole process of convictions and the risk of repeated prosecutions are disproportionate to ensure that he performs military service.[56] The Court also illustrated its argument on the repeated prosecutions as follows:

> they are aimed more at repressing the applicant's intellectual personality, inspiring in him feelings of fear, anguish and vulnerability capable of humiliating and debasing him and breaking his resistance and will. The clandestine life, amounting almost to 'civil death', which the applicant has been compelled to adopt is incompatible with the punishment regime of a democratic society.[57]

The Court considered the repeated prosecution of the applicant to conflict with his intellectual thoughts. By doing so, the Court connected the thoughts of the applicant with his belief. Accordingly, the endless 'circle of military prison–military court–military unit' violates this connection (Cinar 2013: 124). However, it is important to bear in mind that the Court did not refer to the principle of *ne bis in idem*.[58] Furthermore, the conscientious objector's prosecutions, resulting from the conflict between the applicant's conscience and the law, were not examined under the freedom of conscience, thought or religion (Can 2009: 229). As stated by Rachel Brett and Laurel Townhead, 'unfortunately, the Court declined to address the question of whether forcing Ulke performing military service had been a legitimate aim for the state to pursue given his conscientious objection' (Brett and Townhead 2011: 96).

Since recognition of the right to conscientious objection would have meant the recognition of new rights and obligations, the Convention was not interpreted in a broad sense (Muzny 2012: 137–8). Instead, the Court adhered to the Convention's wording without considering the *travaux préparatoires* and the logic behind the text. Thus, until the Grand Chamber's decision in the *Bayatyan v. Armenia* case, the Court relied on Articles 4(3) and 3 of the Convention instead of Article 9 when assessing claims regarding violations against objectors. The Court determined that countries had contravened the Convention because they had not taken the necessary steps to prevent the inhuman treatment and endless prosecution of objectors. However, the Court avoided reaching a conclusion considering Article 9.

Reconsidering the Traditional Approach

The Grand Chamber in the *Bayatyan* case[59] considered whether it was necessary to change the Court's approach to conscientious objection claims. While acknowledging that the Court should not change its precedence without good reason, the Grand Chamber also believed that, as a living instrument, the Convention must be interpreted in a way that promotes the effectiveness of rights protected under the Convention.[60] The Grand Chamber also noted that Article 9 of the Convention has never been applied to conscientious objection claims. Accordingly, as a consequence of interpretation of the issue in the context of Article 4(3), 'conscientious objectors were excluded from the scope of protection of Article 9, which could not be read as guaranteeing freedom from prosecution for refusal to serve in the army'.[61] Highlighting that the Convention is a 'living instrument', the Grand Chamber explicitly refused to comply with the Commission's traditional approach on conscientious objection and abandoned the application of Article 9 in conjunction with Article 4(3).[62] The Grand Chamber was of the opinion that

> Article 9 does not explicitly refer to a right to conscientious objection. However, it considers that opposition to military service, where it is motivated by a serious and insurmountable conflict between the obligation to serve in the army and a person's conscience or his deeply and genuinely held religious or other beliefs, constitutes a conviction or belief of sufficient cogency, seriousness, cohesion and importance to attract the guarantees of Article 9.[63]

The Grand Chamber believed that Bayatyan's objection was grounded on seriously and genuinely held beliefs, given that the applicant belonged to the Jehovah's Witnesses, 'a religious group whose beliefs include the conviction that service, even unarmed, within the military is to be opposed'.[64] Therefore, it found a violation of Article 9. What is striking about the Grand Chamber's decision on *Bayatyan* is that it officially reversed Commission case law and, for the first time, applied Article 9 of the ECHR to evaluate a conscientious objection claim (Muzny 2012: 140). The Grand Chamber explained the reason for such a groundbreaking shift in Court case law as follows:

> almost all the member States which ever had or still have compulsory military service introduced laws at various points recognizing and implementing the right to conscientious objection, some of them even before becoming members of the Council of Europe.[65]

The Court adopted a similar approach in its later decisions on several cases such as *Ercep v. Turkey, Demirtas v. Turkey, Tarhan v. Turkey* and *Savda v. Turkey*. In the case of *Ercep v. Turkey*,[66] the applicant was a Jehovah's Witness. The Court reiterated its *Bayatyan* decision and stated that since no alternative service was provided, the applicant had no choice but to refuse compulsory military service. As a result, the applicant was exposed to repeated prosecutions and imprisonments, which amounted to his 'civil death'.[67] Given that the applicant did not refuse to perform civilian service but asked for an opportunity to do so, the Court had no doubt that the applicant refused to serve because of his sincerely and genuinely held beliefs.[68] The Court ruled that current compulsory military service places a heavy burden on citizens. The system not only deprives citizens of the right to conscientious objection but also imposes criminal sanctions on them.[69] Therefore, the Court concluded that there is no balance between such a system and the general interests of conscientious objectors, and there had been a violation of Article 9.[70]

In *Demirtas v. Turkey*,[71] the Court also believed that the applicant, a Jehovah's Witness, asked for exemption not because he aimed to gain personal benefit but because he held sincere religious beliefs against performing military service. By asking for an alternative form of service, the applicant clearly illustrated that he was ready to share the burden with other citizens. However, the applicant was imprisoned because no alternative service was provided. The Court believed that the state failed to strike a balance between society's general interest and that of objectors. Therefore, the restrictions on the right to religion violated Article 9.

In *Tarhan v. Turkey*,[72] the applicant referred to Ulke's case and asserted that he was subjected to repeated prosecutions and convictions due to the lack of legal protection. He also argued that there was still a risk of prosecution.[73] Acknowledging that, in addition to the current conviction, the applicant was convicted twice previously because of his objection,[74] the Court noted that the Turkish state referred to the right and the duty of states to protect 'territorial integrity, national security, and the rights of others', but failed to explain why, how and to what extent such a right and a duty prevents states from recognising the right to conscientious objection.[75] Regarding the lack of procedures to assess the applicant's status as an objector, the Court also reiterated the cases of *Bayatyan, Ercep* and *Demirtas*, in which all the applicants were Jehovah's Witnesses. For the Court, there was no doubt about the applicants' sincerity in these cases because they were members of a religious group that forbids serving in the army.[76] Yet, in the present case, the applicant did not assert any religious beliefs to support his objection. Therefore, the extent to which

Tarhan's objection to military service fell within the ambit of Article 9 needed to be investigated.[77] Despite this necessity, there was a lack of procedures to assess the applicant's claims. In addition, the authorities penalised the applicant rather than assessing his claims to conscientious objector status.[78] Considering the above-mentioned circumstances, the Court emphasised that the authorities have a positive obligation to protect the applicant's rights under Article 9 of the Convention and to assess whether he is eligible for conscientious objector status. In this sense, the lack of an alternative service and effective procedures to determine the applicant's status breached Article 9 of the Convention.[79] The Court apparently did not assess Tarhan's objection status but focused on the state's positive obligation: that is, to provide the necessary procedures to determine whether the applicant's conscience and belief fell within the scope of Article 9.

In the *Savda v. Turkey* case,[80] the applicant claimed that the criminal sanctions imposed on him owing to his refusal constituted a violation of Articles 9 and 10 of the Convention. The Court focused on similar issues as in the *Tarhan* case, particularly the absence of an alternative service and a procedure to examine objectors' status. The Court held that

> a system which provided for no alternative service or any effective and accessible procedure by which the person concerned was able to have examined the question of whether he could benefit from the right to conscientious objection failed to strike the proper balance between the general interest of society and that of conscientious objectors. It followed that the relevant authorities had failed to comply with their obligation under Article 9 of the Convention.[81]

The Right to Conscientious Objection and Article 14 of the ECHR

Discrimination Between Religious and Non-religious Conscientious Objectors

International documents specifically prohibit any discrimination against conscientious objectors. For instance, the United Nations Human Rights Council asserts in Resolution 24/17 that 'states, in their law and in practice, must not discriminate against conscientious objectors in relation to their terms or conditions of service, or any economic, social, cultural, civil or political rights'.[82] The Human Rights Committee also states in General Comment No. 22 that 'there shall be no discrimination against conscientious objectors because they have failed to perform military service'.[83] Furthermore, in order to provide equal protection to religious claims, states shall make religious privileges available to other beliefs as well unless they have 'reasonable and objective' justifications (Temperman 2010: 204). The UN Human Rights Commission Resolution 1998/77[84] also states that 'conscientious objection to military service derives from principles and reasons of conscience, including profound convictions, arising from religious, ethical, humanitarian or similar motives'.[85] It also calls upon states to take 'account of the requirement not to discriminate amongst conscientious objectors on the basis of their particular beliefs'.[86] Similarly, the Human Rights Committee states in General Comment No. 22 that 'when this right is recognized by law or practice, there shall be no differentiation among conscientious objectors on the basis of the nature of their particular beliefs'.[87] Thus, 'moral, ethical, philosophical and humanitarian, as well as religious, values must be protected with a right to conscientious objection' in an equal way (Wolff 1982: 70).

The European Court also indicated that the protection of Article 9 is not limited to religious motives in its decisions. In *Kokkinakis v. Greece*,[88] the Court highlighted the importance of having the right to freedom of religion, conscience and thought in a democratic society. According to the Court,

> as enshrined in Article 9 (art. 9), freedom of thought, conscience and religion is one of the foundations of a 'democratic society' within the meaning of the Convention. It is, in its religious dimension, one of the most vital elements that go to make up the identity of believers and their conception of life, but it is also a precious asset for atheists, agnostics, sceptics and the unconcerned.[89]

As this passage illustrates, the protection of Article 9 is not restricted to recognition of a particular religion. In the case of a conscientious objection based on the right to freedom of thought, conscience and religion, it is clear that although well-known religious groups – namely, Jehovah's Witnesses and Quakers – are granted exemption from military service, conscientious objection is not exclusively limited to those religiously motivated groups (Leigh and Born 2008: 74). Despite the differences in the motivations behind their refusal, both Quakers (refusing to serve in the army based on their membership of a religious group that condemns war) and individuals (refusing to serve in the army based on personal motives) have a common denominator for their refusal, which is the 'horror of war' (Cohen and Greenspan 1967: 403). Both religious and ethical objectors condemn the use of force and oppose war in general. While religious objectors base their decision on the 'Supreme Being's command', ethical objectors rely on the idea that 'love of humanity' does not allow the use of violence against human beings. Therefore, differentiating between religious objectors and ethical objectors is 'unreasonable' (Donnici 1964: 39).

As indicated by David Cohen and Robert Greenspan (1967: 403), 'nothing is more repugnant to a sense of fairness than the rejection of the claim of a conscientious objector because [s]he does not believe in a transcendent reality'. Conscience is not necessarily a result of a religious belief. Many individuals behave in accordance with their conscience rather than following religious dictates. Therefore, conscientious objection status might be granted based on convictions that are not religiously held but 'possess a reverence for human life; a belief in the transcendency of love and global brotherhood; a convincement in a principle of goodness; or a steadfast belief that human life is sacred and should not be humanly terminated' (Wolff 1982: 69–70).

In addition to the discrimination between non-religious and religious conscientious objectors, there has been disagreement on why traditional religious groups obtain exemption more easily than minority religious groups. Whereas members of minority religions[90] might have difficulties explaining their motives to the Convention institutions within the European Convention system, the motives of members affiliated with dominant religions[91] are accepted without a burden of proof (Ahdar and Leigh 2005: 124). In *N v. Sweden,*[92] the applicant sought total exemption from military service owing to his pacifist views. In his letter to the government explaining his reasons for not complying with the military order, the applicant asked, 'why is it that total resistance is only accepted if you adhere to the Jehovah's Witnesses?' The applicant alleged before the Commission that 'while members of Jehovah's Witnesses are exempted from military service and thus not sentenced',[93] his conviction for evasion breached Article 14 of the Convention in conjunction with Article 9. The Commission favoured that the complaint of discrimination fell within the ambit of the right to freedom of religion. However, the only issue on which the Commission decided was whether differentiating between Jehovah's Witnesses and the applicant in granting total exemption from military service has an 'objective and reasonable justification under Article 14 of the Convention'.[94] In this regard, the Commission noted that membership of the Jehovah's Witnesses requires a 'comprehensive set of rules of behaviour' which includes the refusal of military service and any alternative service. Furthermore, being a member of the Jehovah's Witnesses 'constitutes strong evidence that the objections to compulsory service are based on genuine religious convictions. No comparable evidence exists in regard to individuals who object to compulsory service without being members of a community with similar characteristics.'[95] The Commission, therefore, found that

> membership of such a religious sect as Jehovah's Witnesses is an objective fact which creates a high degree of probability that exemption is not granted to persons who simply wish to escape service, since it is unlikely that a person would join such a sect only for the purpose of not having to perform military or substitute service. The same high probability would not exist if exemption was also granted to individuals claiming to have objections of conscience to such service or to members of various pacifist groups or organizations.[96]

In conclusion, the right to conscientious objection was initially granted restrictedly to those refusing military service because of their religious beliefs. Some countries even required objectors to be affiliated with a certain church or specific religious organisations (Weissbrodt 1988: 53). This narrow approach on conscientious objection 'neglects the human ability to form personal opinions and interpret their espoused religion in an individualized way' (Marcus 1997: 540). Yet, by the end of the nineteenth century, conscience started to be considered a legitimate ground for claiming the right to conscientious objection. As such, non-religious objectors, particularly antimilitarists and political objectors, began to claim the right to conscientious objection. As seen above, being a member of a well-established religion was not the only condition for obtaining exemption from military service (Bröckling 2009: 53). As a result of both the efforts of international organisations and the complaints of individuals, the concept of conscientious objection was broadened. Countries started to recognise the right of those who based their objection to military service on sincere ethical grounds. Furthermore, a few countries broadened the definition of conscientious objection to include refusals based on beliefs such as the use of nuclear weapons being illegal (Weissbrodt 1988: 53–4).

Different Treatment for Conscientious Law-Breakers?
As the Human Rights Committee states, 'convicted conscientious objectors bear the stigma of a criminal record'.[97] As a result, objectors do not fully enjoy their social and economic rights.[98] In *Thlimmenos v. Greece*,[99] the European Court (Grand Chamber) considered whether the failure to differentiate between conscientious objectors and other law-breakers constitutes discrimination. The applicant was a Jehovah's Witness, convicted of insubordination for refusing to wear a military uniform and

sentenced to four years' imprisonment.[100] After several years, he passed a public examination which allows candidates to become chartered accountants. Despite his success, the Executive Board of the Greek Institute of Chartered Accountants refused his application because he was previously 'convicted of a serious crime'.[101] The applicant alleged that Greek law excludes all persons convicted of a serious crime from becoming a chartered accountant without distinguishing between conscientious law-breakers and others convicted of serious crimes.[102] According to the applicant, excluding an individual from the profession because they refused to do military service based on their religious belief has no useful purpose. The nature of the offence and the motive of offenders should be considered. The government failed to consider the differences between individuals refusing military service because of their right to freedom of religion and others who committed serious crimes.[103] Accordingly, the Court stated that

> the Court has so far considered that the right under Article 14 not to be discriminated against in the enjoyment of the rights guaranteed under the Convention is violated when States treat differently persons in analogous situations without providing an objective and reasonable justification (see the Inze judgment cited above, p. 18, § 41). The Court considers that this is not the only facet of the prohibition of discrimination in Article 14. The right not to be discriminated against in the enjoyment of the rights guaranteed under the Convention is also violated when States without an objective and reasonable justification fail to treat differently persons whose situations are significantly different.[104]

The Court revised its approach towards the principle of equality. It interpreted the equality principle in a broader sense. Accordingly, in addition to identical treatment when necessary, the principle of equality requires a difference in treatment. Therefore, giving the same treatment to persons who experience different situations is now considered as violating the right not to be discriminated against (Martínez-Torrón 2001: 194). In other words, the breath-taking feature of this judgement is that identical treatment is now considered as a violation of the state's responsibility to provide different treatment for those who have special circumstances. The *Thlimmenos* judgement, clear enough to be considered a principle, indicates that the prohibition of discrimination requires states to differentiate, if necessary (Edel 2010: 64–6). In conclusion, this kind of criminal conviction could be characterised as a matter of conscience. Therefore, individuals convicted on the grounds of their conscience should be able to claim exemption from the general rule, which excludes those convicted of serious crimes from gaining certain benefits (Martínez-Torrón 2001: 194–5).

The Right to Conscientious Objection and United Nations Human Rights Law

The Right to Conscientious Objection and Article 18 of the ICCPR

Given the lack of explicit recognition of the right to conscientious objection at the international level, the right to freedom of religion, conscience and thought constitutes one of the fundamental rights that give rise to the right to conscientious objection. The right to religion, conscience and thought in the light of the ECHR and the case law of the ECtHR was examined in the previous section; this section now examines the right to conscientious objection under United Nations Human Rights Law. The question that has to be considered here is whether Article 18 of the Covenant, which protects the right to freedom of religion, thought and conscience, constitutes a ground for recognition of the right to conscientious objection. To start with the wording of Article 18 of the Covenant, Article 18(1) reads as follows:

> Everyone shall have the right to freedom of thought, conscience and religion. This right shall include freedom to have or to adopt a religion or belief of [their] choice, and freedom, either individually or in community with others and in public or private, to manifest [their] religion or belief in worship, observance, practice and teaching.[105]

This Article's relevance to the right to conscientious objection is that religions mostly adopt non-violent principles strictly forbidding killing. Some of them forbid people even to be involved in actions contradicting the requirements of being a member of these religions. Therefore, the protection of religion without enabling the right to be exempted from such obligations that contradict their belief is not adequate. Article 18 of the Covenant protects manifestation of 'religion or belief in worship, observance, practice and teaching'. This gives meaning to the individual's inward feelings and helps individuals put their belief into action (Wolff 1982: 84–5). Similarly, the explicit protection of observance and practice in Article 18(1) of the ICCPR illustrates that individuals should not be compelled to act against their convictions. The mere recognition of a right to hold a conscientious belief that forbids one from taking a human life is not satisfactory. The practical importance of the right to conscience is understood when it allows 'satisfying one's convictions'. Therefore, it can be said that the main aim of recognising the right to conscientious objection is to guarantee properly the right to conscience (Wolff 1982: 82). Furthermore, Article 18(2) reads as follows: '[n]o one shall be subject to coercion which would impair his[her] freedom to have or to adopt a religion or belief of his[her] choice'.[106] In this context, coercing individuals into serving in the army clearly violates Article 18(2) of the Covenant. Most importantly, the right to conscientious objection constitutes the very essence of the right to religion, thought and conscience and 'the true impact of the right occurs when individuals do not have to act in contradiction to their convictions' (Wolff 1982: 82).

Development of the Right to Conscientious Objection under the UN Bodies

Resolutions and General Comments

In its Resolution 33/165 on the status of persons refusing service in military or police forces used to enforce apartheid,[107] the General Assembly 'recognizes the right of all persons to refuse service in military or police forces which are used to enforce apartheid'.[108] Similarly, the Commission on Human Rights, in its Resolution 1987/46,

> recognizing that conscientious objection to military service derives from principles and reasons of conscience, including profound convictions, arising from religious, ethical, moral or similar motives,
>
> 1. Appeals to States to recognize that conscientious objection to military service should be considered a legitimate exercise of the right to freedom of thought, conscience and religion recognized by the Universal Declaration of Human Rights and the International Covenant on Civil and Political Rights.
> 2. Invites States to take measures aimed at exemption from military service on the basis of a genuinely held conscientious objection to armed service.[109]

The Commission on Human Rights, in its Resolution 1995/83, recalls Resolution 1989/59, in which it held that everyone should be allowed

> to have conscientious objections to military service as a legitimate exercise of the right of freedom of thought, conscience and religion as laid down in Article 18 of the Universal Declaration of Human Rights as well as Article 18 of the International Covenant on Civil and Political Rights.[110]

It also 'appeals to States to take necessary steps to accommodate the exemption from military service'.[111] Furthermore, in its General Comment No. 22, the Human Rights Committee stated that

> many individuals have claimed the right to refuse to perform military service (conscientious objection) on the basis that such right derives from their freedoms under article 18. In response to such claims, a growing number of States have in their laws exempted from compulsory military service citizens who genuinely hold religious or other beliefs that forbid the performance of military service and replaced it with alternative national service. The Covenant does not explicitly refer to a right to conscientious objection, but the Committee believes that such a right can be derived from article 18, inasmuch as the obligation to use lethal force may seriously conflict with the freedom of conscience and the right to manifest one's religion or belief.[112]

The main question before the Committee in the draft of General Comment No. 22 was whether the Committee would completely revise its initial standpoint and recognise Article 18 of the Covenant as a ground for the right to conscientious objection. By referring to 'the obligation to use lethal force', the Committee seems to prefer a middle view. In this sense, the Committee recognises the right to conscientious objection, yet it limits the enjoyment of that right to cases that require individuals to use lethal force (Takemura 2009: 60).

It is also important to consider that applying for conscientious objection status is not limited to exemption claims raised before joining the army. As the United Nations Human Rights Council states, 'persons performing military service may develop conscientious objections'.[113] Individuals might decide to be conscientious objectors during their service in the armed forces. It might be a result of changing religion or facing a specific problem while serving in the army. Therefore, conscientious objection status cannot be limited to those who have not joined the army.[114]

Reconsidering the Traditional Approach

In its initial decisions, the Human Rights Committee adopted a traditional approach and concluded that Article 18 of the Covenant does not protect the right to conscientious objection to military service. The reason behind this traditional approach was either a lack of explicit recognition of the right to conscientious objection or vague interpretations of Article 8 of the Convention.[115] In *L.T.K. v. Finland*,[116] the applicant, who 'informed the authorities of his ethical convictions and of his desire to perform only alternative service',[117] claimed that refusal of conscientious objection status and prosecutions against him violated his right to religion, thought and conscience under Article 18 of the Covenant.[118] The Committee, however, focused on Article 8 of the Covenant, which excludes 'any service of a military character and, in countries where conscientious objection is recognized, any national service required by law of conscientious objectors' from 'forced or compulsory labour'. It decided that '[t]he Covenant does not provide for the right to conscientious objection; neither Article 18 nor Article 19 of the Covenant'.[119]

A shift from the traditional approach to a wider interpretation of Article 18 of the Covenant can be seen in the Committee's later decisions.[120] Due to consistent individual complaints, the Committee revised its decision and protected the right to conscientious objection under Article 18 of the Covenant (Takemura 2009: 69). In *J. P. v. Canada*,[121] while the Committee refused to recognise exemption claims regarding taxes as part of the rights protected under Article 18 of the Covenant, it reached a conclusion that 'Article 18 of the Covenant certainly protects the right to hold, express and disseminate opinions and convictions, including conscientious objection to military activities'.[122] This clearly indicates that the Committee departed from its previous decisions in which Article 18 of the Covenant was interpreted to mean that it does not protect the right to conscientious objection (Major 2001: 15).

In *Paul Westerman v. the Netherlands*,[123] the question before the Committee was whether compulsory military service violates the author's right to freedom of conscience. Although the Committee refers to General Comment No. 22, which recognises Article 18 of the Covenant as a legal ground for claiming the right to conscientious objection, it ruled that the author failed to prove that his objection was 'insurmountable'.[124] Yet, in the dissenting opinion, the Committee members considered the different aspects of General Comment No. 22. They reminded us that discrimination against conscientious objection is prohibited under paragraph 11 of General Comment No. 22. Accordingly, the state's failure to provide 'justification for its decision to interfere with the author's right under Article 18 of the Covenant in the form of denial of conscientious objector's status and imposing a term of imprisonment' violates Article 18 of the Covenant.[125] This dissent, which interpreted General Comment No. 22 from a different angle, raises awareness of all forms of discrimination against conscientious objectors. It also shows a tendency to recognise the right to conscientious objection (Kessler 2013: 783).

Similarly, in *Yeo-Bum Yoon and Myung-Jin Choi v. Republic of Korea*,[126] in which the authors claimed that the absence of an alternative civil service breaches Article 18 of the Covenant,[127] the Committee decided for the first time that the lack of an alternative civil service does breach Article 18 (Kessler 2013: 783). The Committee reversed its decision in *L. T. K. v. Finland* and expressed the view that 'Article 8 of the Covenant itself neither recognizes nor excludes a right of conscientious objection'.[128] The Committee further recalled paragraph 4 of its General Comment No. 22, which expresses the opinion that

> to compel a person to use lethal force, although such use would seriously conflict with the requirements of his conscience or religious beliefs, falls within the ambit of Article 18. The Committee notes, in the instant case, that the authors' refusal to be drafted for compulsory service was a direct expression of their religious beliefs, which it is uncontested were genuinely held. The authors' conviction and sentence, accordingly, amounts to a restriction on their ability to manifest their religion or belief. Such restriction must be justified by the permissible limits described in paragraph 3 of Article 18, that is, that any restriction must be prescribed by law and be necessary to protect public safety, order, health or morals or the fundamental rights and freedoms of others. However, such restriction must not impair the very essence of the right in question.[129]

The question raised before the Committee was whether these restrictions are compatible with Article 18(3) of the Covenant and have a legitimate ground.[130] Considering the arguments of the state party on the necessity of restrictions on Article 18 of the Covenant in the name of protection of public safety, the Committee focused on the fact that a large number of state parties introduced an alternative service into their legal systems and considered that 'the State party has failed to show what special disadvantage would be involved for it if the rights of the authors under Article 18 would be fully respected'.[131] The Committee, therefore, concluded that the failure of the state party to introduce an alternative civil service violates Article 18 of the Covenant.

Conclusion

Since the right to conscientious objection has not been recognised as an independent right in the international arena, it is important to consider that the right to conscientious objection derives from the right to freedom of thought, conscience and religion, which has been recognised in international treaties and organisations. While the traditional interpretation of the ECHR by the ECtHR was that the Convention's text does not protect the right to conscientious objection, individuals continued to bring cases to the ECtHR, alleging that refusing to enable individuals to assert the right to conscientious objection is a violation of Article 9 of the ECHR. These attempts forced states to recognise the right to conscientious objection and, as such, there has been a significant change in the position of the ECtHR on the recognition of the right to conscientious objection.

Notes

1. United Nation Economic and Social Council, 'Report of the Office of the High Commissioner for Human Rights, Civil and Political Rights, Including the Question of Conscientious Objection to Military Service, U.N. Doc. E/CN.4/2004/55 (16 February 2004)' para.38(c).
2. Council of Europe: Committee of Ministers, 'Recommendation No. R (87) 8 of the Committee of Ministers to Member States Regarding Conscientious Objection to Compulsory Military Service' para.1. Available at: <http://www.refworld.org/docid/5069778e2.html> (last accessed 14 April 2017).
3. Council of Europe: Parliamentary Assembly, 'Recommendation 1518 (2001): Exercise of the Right of Conscientious Objection to Military Service in Council of Europe Member States' para.2. Available at: <http://www.refworld.org/docid/5107cf8f2.html> (last accessed 14 April 2017).
4. European Convention on Human Rights, 3 September 1953, Article 9.
5. *Campbell and Cosans v. the United Kingdom* App. No. 7511/76; 7743/76 (ECtHR, 25 February 1982) at para.36.
6. One way of testing exemption claims is the 'subjective-functional approach'. Within this approach, the questions that are bound to arise include: 'does the claimant himself or herself *subjectively* believe in the things or persons at the centre of their faiths?' and 'does the belief system *function* as a religion in the individual's life?' (see Ahdar and Leigh 2005: 115). See also the *United States v. Seeger* and *Welsh v. United States* cases, in which the Court applied the subjective-functional approach in order to determine applicants' exemption claims. In these cases, the main issue was 'to decide whether the beliefs professed by a registrant are sincerely held and whether they are, in his own scheme of things, religious' (see 380 U.S. 163, 164).
7. *Eweida and Others v. the UK* App. Nos. 48420/10, 59842/10, 51671/10 and 36516/10 (ECtHR, 27 May 2013).
8. For further discussion, see Evans (2003: 76).
9. *Eweida and Others v. the UK* App. Nos. 48420/10, 59842/10, 51671/10 and 36516/10 (ECtHR, 27 May 2013) at Partially Dissenting Opinion of Judges Vucinic and De Gaetano at para.3.
10. Partially Dissenting Opinion of Judges Vucinic and De Gaetano at para.2.
11. *Darby v. Sweden* App. No. 11581/85 (ECtHR, 23 October 1990); *Valsamis v. Greece* App. No. 21787/93 (ECtHR, 18 December 1996); *Efstratiou v. Greece* App. No. 24095/94 (ECtHR, 18 December 1996).
12. European Convention on Human Rights, 3 September 1953, Article 9(1).

13. Article 18 of the UDHR reads as follows: 'Everyone has the right to freedom of thought, conscience and religion; this right includes freedom to change his religion or belief, and freedom, either alone or in community with others and in public or private, to manifest his religion or belief in teaching, practice, worship and observance.'

14. *Arrowsmith v. the United Kingdom* App. No. 7050/75 (European Commission of Human Rights, 5 December 1978) at para.2.

15. Ibid. at para.69.

16. Ibid. at para.71.

17. *Valsamis v. Greece* App. No. 21787/93 (ECtHR, 18 December 1996).

18. Ibid. at para.8.

19. Ibid. at para.6.

20. Ibid. at para.9.

21. Ibid. at para.10.

22. Ibid. at para.34.

23. However, in the dissenting opinion the Judge said that: 'Victoria Valsamis stated that the parade she did not participate in had a character and symbolism that were clearly contrary to her neutralist, pacifist, and thus religious, beliefs. We are of the opinion that the Court has to accept that and we find no basis for seeing Victoria's participation in this parade as necessary in a democratic society, even if this public event clearly was for most people an expression of national values and unity.'

24. Ibid. at para.37.

25. Separate opinion of Mr Opsahl in *Arrowsmith v. the United Kingdom* App. No. 7050/75 (European Commission on Human Rights, 5 December 1978) at para.2.

26. *Eweida and Others v. the UK* App. Nos. 48420/10, 59842/10, 51671/10 and 36516/10 (ECtHR, 27 May 2013).

27. Ibid. at para.58.

28. Ibid. at para.82.

29. Ibid. in Partly Dissenting Opinion of Judges Bratza and David Thór Björgvinsson.

30. *Jakobski v. Poland* App. No. 18429/06 (ECtHR, 7 December 2010) at para.7.

31. Ibid. at para.30.

32. Ibid. at para.27.

33. Ibid. at para.45.

34. Ibid. at para.45.

35. Ibid. at para.46.

36. *Campbell and Cosans v. the United Kingdom* App. Nos. 7511/76, 7743/76 (ECtHR, 25 February 1982).

37. *Grandrath v. Germany* App. No. 229964/10 (European Commission, 12 October 1966).

38. Ibid. at para.9.

39. Ibid. at para.32.

40. Ibid. at para.32.

41. *Bayatyan v. Armenia* App. No. 23459/03 (ECtHR, 27 October 2009).

42. Ibid. at para.3
43. Ibid. at para.55.
44. *X v. Austria* App. No. 5591/72 (European Commission, 2 April 1973).
45. Ibid., cited in *Bayatyan v. Armenia* App. No. 23459/03 (ECtHR, 27 October 2009) at para.56.
46. *Ulke v. Turkey* App. No. 39437/98 (ECtHR, 24 April 2004) at [53-54] cited in *Bayatyan v. Armenia* App. No. 23459/03 (ECtHR, 27 October 2009) at para.59.
47. *Ulke v. Turkey* App. No. 39437/98 (ECtHR, 24 April 2004) [63-64] cited in *Bayatyan v. Armenia* App. No. 23459/03 (ECtHR, 27 October 2009) at para.59.
48. Ibid. at para.60.
49. *Ulke v. Turkey* App. No. 39437/98 (ECtHR, 24 April 2004).
50. Ibid. at para.48.
51. 'When Osman Murat Ulke was called up for military service he refused to join the army. He publicly burned the call-up papers in 1995. A year later he was arrested and charged under Article 155 of the Penal Code and Article 58 of the Military Penal Code. In a decision of 28 January 1997, the General Staff Court in Ankara sentenced him to six months' imprisonment. Meanwhile, Osman Murat Ulke had been transferred on 22 November 1996 to the Bilecik gendarmerie command. Because of his refusal to wear a military uniform, he was detained, and he also refused to wear the prison uniform. On 26 November 1996, the military prosecutor charged him with "persistent disobedience" under Article 87 of the Military Penal Code. He was convicted again and sentenced to five months' imprisonment. When released on 27 December 1996, he did not rejoin his regiment. He was arrested and detained pending trial and charged with desertion and "persistent disobedience". He received a sentence of ten months' imprisonment and a fine in October 1997 spending 701 days in imprisonment as a result of eight separate convictions' (Boyle 2009: 213).
52. Ibid. at para.48.
53. Ibid. at para.59.
54. Ibid. at para.60.
55. Ibid. at para.61.
56. Ibid. at para.62.
57. Ibid. at para.62.
58. *Ne bis in idem* is a Latin term with the literal meaning 'not twice about the same'.
59. *Bayatyan v. Armenia* Grand Chamber App. No. 23459/03 (ECtHR, 7 July 2011).
60. Ibid. at para.98.
61. Ibid. at para.99.
62. Ibid. at para.109.
63. Ibid. at para.110.
64. Ibid. at para.111.
65. Ibid. at para.46.
66. *Ercep v. Turkey* App. No. 43965/04 (ECtHR, 22 November 2011).
67. Ibid. at para.58.
68. Ibid. at para.61.

69. Ibid. at para.63.
70. Ibid. at paras.64,65.
71. *Feti Demirtas v. Turkey* App. No. 5260/07 (ECtHR, 17 January 2012).
72. *Tarhan v. Turkey* App. No. 9078/06 (ECtHR, 17 July 2012).
73. Ibid. at para.34.
74. Ibid. at para.36.
75. Ibid. at para.56.
76. Ibid. at para.57.
77. Ibid. at para.58.
78. Ibid. at para.59.
79. Ibid. at para.61.
80. *Savda v. Turkey* App. No. 42730/05 (ECtHR, 12 June 2012).
81. European Court of Human Rights, 'Refusal to Grant Conscientious Objector Status is not Necessary in a Democratic Society. Press Release, ECHR 250 (2012)'. Available at: <http://www.ebco-beoc.org/sites/ebcobeoc.org/files/attachments/PR_Chamber%20II%20judgment%20Savda%20v.%20Turkey%2012.06.2012.pdf> (last accessed 19 September 2017).
82. United Nations Human Rights Council, 'Conscientious Objection to Military Service: Resolution 24/17 (8 October 2013) A/HRC/RES/24/17' para.12.
83. United Nations Human Rights Committee, 'CCPR General Comment No. 22: Article 18 (Freedom of Thought, Conscience or Religion), 30 July 1993, CCPR/C/21/Rev.1/Add.4', para.11. Available at: <http://www.refworld.org/docid/453883fb22.html> (last accessed 14 April 2017).
84. United Nations Commission on Human Rights, 'Conscientious Objection to Military Service: Resolution 1998/77 (22 April 1998) E/CN.4/RES/1998/77'.
85. Ibid.
86. Ibid. at para.3.
87. United Nations Human Rights Committee, 'CCPR General Comment No. 22: Article 18 (Freedom of Thought, Conscience or Religion), 30 July 1993, CCPR/C/21/Rev.1/Add.4', para.11. Available at: <http://www.refworld.org/docid/453883fb22.html> (last accessed 14 April 2017).
88. *Kokkinakis v. Greece* App. No. 14307/88 (ECtHR, 25 May1993).
89. Ibid. at para.31.
90. See *X v. United Kingdom* App. No. 7291/75 (1977) and *X v. Federal Republic of Germany* App. No. 445/70, (1970).
91. See *Chappell v. United Kingdom* App. No. 12587/86 (1987).
92. *N v. Sweden* App. No. 10410/83 (European Commission, 11 October 1984).
93. Ibid.
94. Ibid.
95. Ibid.
96. Ibid.
97. United Nations Human Rights Committee, 'Consideration of Reports Submitted by State Parties under Article 40 of the Covenant: Concluding Observations of the Human Rights Committee: Republic of Korea (28 November 2006) CCPR/C/KOR/CO/3' para.17.

98. In the case of Atasoy and Sarkut, one of the applicants, 'Mr Sarkut, due to an order sent by military officials to his employer in November 2008, has lost his employment as a teacher' (para.8.1). The university was advised not to re-employ the author unless he provided a document from the Military Recruitment Office. In the event that the university did re-employ him, it would be accused of having committed a crime under, inter alia, articles 91, 92 and 93 of Military Law No. 1111' (para.2.6). The Committee notes the authors' claim that their rights under Article 18, paragraph 1, of the Covenant have been violated, due to the absence in the State party of an alternative to compulsory military service, as a result of which, they have been criminally prosecuted due to their failure to perform military service, with Mr. Sarkut having lost his employment' (para.10.2).

99. *Thlimmenos v. Greece* App. No. 34369/97 (ECtHR, 6 April 2000).

100. Ibid. at para.7.

101. Ibid. at para.8.

102. Ibid. at para.33.

103. Ibid. at para.34.

104. Ibid. at para.44.

105. International Covenant on Civil and Political Rights, 19 December 1966, Article 18(1).

106. International Covenant on Civil and Political Rights, 19 December 1966, Article 18(2).

107. United Nations General Assembly, 'Status of Persons Refusing Service in Military or Police Forces Used to Enforce Apartheid 20 December 1978, A/RES/33/165'. Available at: <http://www.refworld.org/docid/3b00f1ae28.html> (last accessed 14 April 2017).

108. Ibid. at para.1.

109. United Nations Commission on Human Rights, 'Conscientious Objection to Military Service (10 March 1987) E/CN.4/RES/1987/46'. Available at: <http://www.refworld.org/docid/3b00f0ce50.html> (last accessed 21 May 2017).

110. United Nations Commission on Human Rights, 'Conscientious Objection to Military Service (8 March 1995) E/CN.4/RES/1995/83' para.1. Available at: <http://www.refworld.org/docid/3b00f0d220.html> (last accessed 21 May 2017).

111. Ibid. at para.2.

112. United Nations Human Rights Committee, 'CCPR General Comment No. 22: Article 18 (Freedom of Thought, Conscience or Religion), 30 July 1993, CCPR/C/21/Rev.1/Add.4', para.11. Available at: <http://www.refworld.org/docid/453883fb22.html> (last accessed 14 April 2017).

113. United Nations Human Rights Council, 'Conscientious Objection to Military Service (23 September 2013) A/HRC/24/L.23'. Available at: <http://www.refworld.org/docid/526e3e114.html> (last accessed 21 May 2017).

114. Quaker United Nations Office, 'International Standards on Conscientious Objection to Military Service' (November 2011). Available at: <https://www.refworld.org/docid/4f0564862.html> (last accessed 16 January 2021).

115. Ibid., p.3.
116. *L. T. K. v. Finland*, Communication No. 185/1984, CCPR/C/OP/2 (1990).
117. Ibid. at para.2.2.
118. Ibid. at para.1.
119. Ibid. at para.5.2.
120. See *Aapo Jarvinen v. Finland; H.A.G.M. Brinkhof v. the Netherlands; Foin v. France, Maille v. France, Venier & Nicolas v. France,* in which the Committee did not find for the requirement for longer alternative civilian service as this would constitute discrimination under Article 26 of the Covenant.
121. *J. P. v. Canada*, Communication No. 446/1991, CCPR/C/43/D/446/1991 (1991).
122. Ibid. at para.4.2.
123. *Paul Westerman v. the Netherlands,* Communication No. 682/1996, CCPR/C/67/D/682/1996 (1999).
124. Ibid. at para.9.
125. Ibid. at Dissenting Opinion by Committee members P. Bhagwati, L. Henkin, C. Medina Quiroga, F. Pocar and M. Scheinin.
126. Human Rights Committee United Nations, 'Yeo-Bum Yoon and Myung-Jin Choi v. Republic of Korea, CCPR/C/88/D/1321-1322/2004' (23 January 2007).
127. Ibid. at para.3.
128. Ibid. at para.8.2. See also *Young-Kwan Kim et al. v. Rep. of Korea* (CCPR/C/112/D/2179/2012 Communication No. 2179/2012 of 14 January 2015) and *Atasoy and Sarkut v. Turkey* (CCPR/ C/104/D/1853-1854/2008 of 19 June 2012).
129. Ibid. at para.8.3.
130. Ibid.
131. Ibid. at para.8.4.

CHAPTER 3

The Compatibility of Turkish Domestic Law with International Law

Introduction

International bodies show an increased tendency towards recognition of the right to conscientious objection, yet implementation of the right varies from one state to another. While some countries have legally recognised conscientious objection and prevent the criminalisation of objectors, others have not (Leigh and Born 2008: 74). The national legislation on compulsory military service in Turkey exemplifies the controversial implementations of the right to conscientious objection well. This chapter, therefore, analyses the non-recognition of the right to conscientious objection in the Turkish domestic legal system and its compatibility with international standards. It first examines the national legislation on military service and significant domestic cases in relation to the right to conscientious objection in Turkey. Then it analyses Turkey's compliance with the international standards[1] on prevention of arbitrary detention of conscientious objectors: namely, the principles of *'ne bis in idem'* and the 'right to fair trial'. Finally, it scrutinises conscientious objection in the light of the right to freedom of expression under Article 10 of ECHR: first, to show the intersection of the right to freedom of expression with the right to religion, thought and conscience, particularly in situations that involve declaring objections to military service and criticising the use of force; and second, to reveal the contradiction between Article 318 of the Turkish Criminal Code and Article 10 of the ECHR.

National Legislation on Compulsory Military Service

Article 72 of the 1982 Constitution, entitled 'national service', states that 'national service is the right and duty of every Turk. The manner in which this service shall be performed, or considered as performed, either in the Armed Forces or in public service shall be regulated by law.'[2] The wording of Article 72 does not reduce national service to military service; whether national service will be performed as 'public service' or 'military service' is open to interpretation. Yet, compulsory military service is imposed as national service through Article 1 of the Law on Military Service Act No. 1111, which states that 'every male Turkish citizen is obliged to perform his military service in accordance with this law'[3]. Moreover, Article 45 of the Military Criminal Code[4] rejects any forms of exemption based on conscientious grounds by ruling that 'individuals may not evade military service, and penalties may not be revoked, for religious or moral reasons'[5].

Unlike Article 72, Article 76 of the Turkish Constitution refers to 'military service'. It rules that those 'who have failed to perform compulsory military service shall not be elected deputies, even if they have been pardoned'.[6] This does not indicate that military service is imposed on Turkish citizens through the Turkish Constitution. On the contrary, one can argue that the Constitution neither imposes compulsory military service nor prevents the recognition of the right to conscientious objection (Üçpınar 2009: 244). However, there is a crucial issue that needs to be considered here: Article 76 still reflects the fact that conscientious objectors in Turkey are, as the Human Rights Committee puts it, 'practically deprived of their civil and political rights such as freedom of movement and right to vote'.[7] Once they have declared their refusal to perform military service, they are deprived of their basic constitutional rights, such as the right to be elected as members of parliament.[8] Thus, they do not enjoy their full civil and political rights.

Article 72 of the Constitution, as argued by Hülya Üçpınar (2009: 244), allows the authorities to regulate how national service is performed, yet it does not stipulate that military service is compulsory. Therefore, Article 1 of the Military Code and Article 45 of the Military Penal Code contradict the Turkish Constitution, which does not impose compulsory military service but recognises the right to freedom of conscience. Üçpınar also points out that this contradiction between the Constitution and the Military Penal Code gives rise to the application of Article 11 on 'Supremacy and Binding Force of the Constitution', which indicates that 'the provisions of the Constitution are fundamental legal rules binding upon legislative, executive and judicial organs, and administrative authorities and other institutions and individuals. Laws shall not be in conflict with the Constitution.'[9] This point was, indeed, raised by one conscientious objector. In the case of Enver Aydemir, the applicant alleged that Article

76 of the Constitution was contrary to the essence of the Constitution; however, the military court rejected the applicant's claim on the grounds that exemption based on religious grounds goes against Article 10 of the Turkish Constitution[10] on equality before the law.[11]

The Right to Conscientious Objection at the Domestic Court

This part of the chapter examines two distinct cases, those of Muhammed Serdar Delice[12] and Enver Aydemir,[13] to demonstrate how domestic courts interpret the right to conscientious objection. To start with the former case, Delice was absent from his regiment between 24 February 2010 and 27 November 2011 and was convicted of desertion under Military Penal Code Article 66/1-a. In his defence before the court, he claimed that he was not a deserter but a conscientious objector. He stated that he left the military in order to declare his objection and became an objector. Before examining his situation, the military court considered the international standards on conscientious objection. The military court cited Resolution 337 (1967) of the Parliamentary Assembly of the Council of Europe on the right to conscientious objection, which states that:

1. Persons liable to conscription for military service who, for reasons of conscience or profound conviction arising from religious, ethical, moral, humanitarian, philosophical or similar motives, refuse to perform armed service shall enjoy a personal right to be released from the obligation to perform such service.
2. This right shall be regarded as deriving logically from the fundamental rights of the individual in democratic Rule of Law States which are guaranteed in Article 9 of the European Convention on Human Rights.[14]

Furthermore, in the present case, the military court highlighted that the claims regarding the right to conscientious objection were examined in the context of Articles 3 and 14 instead of Article 9 of the ECHR. However, the military court admitted that after the *Bayatyan* case, the European Court applied Article 9 of the Convention and interpreted the right to conscientious objection in line with the 'living instrument' approach, which requires the Convention to be interpreted in light of present-day conditions. The military court also considered that although the right to conscientious objection is not recognised at the national level, Article 90 of the Constitution requires the domestic courts to consider such international rules.[15]

The military court referred, then, to the *Bayatyan* case, in which the European Court applied Article 9 of the Convention and admitted that, under Article 90 of the Turkish Constitution, judges are required to consider international rules. Yet, the Court did not recognise Delice as an objector. According to the military court, Delice served in the military for five months without any objection based on religious beliefs. The Court argued that his beliefs were not expressed until after he had joined and accepted the military service despite his beliefs (see Chapters 4 and 5 for Delice's own interpretation of how he decided to become an objector). The military court concluded that although, as explained in the *Bayatyan* case, the right to conscientious objection is derived from the right to religion, conscience and thought, and this interpretation could be applied to domestic law as well, the right to conscientious objection does not mean that each individual could assert it based on personal reasons: it is, rather, a right that can be enjoyed through their membership of a group such as the Jehovah's Witnesses. Individuals are entitled to demand this right based on membership of a group that essentially refused military service. However, according to the military court, Delice subscribed to Islam (a religion that does not refuse military service) and became an objector after witnessing the good and bad sides of military life during his five months of service. Therefore, his claim was rejected on the grounds that Delice could not prove that his objection to military service was motivated by his religious beliefs, which were 'genuinely held and were in serious and insurmountable conflict with his obligation to perform military service'.[16]

In the case of Delice, the military court referred for the first time to an international case with an explicit reference to Article 90 of the Turkish Constitution. According to Delice's lawyer, 'this decision is a precedent for all trials related to conscientious objection' (Karaca 2012). His lawyer also stated that:

> for the first time, the European Commission, the European Convention on Human Rights and decisions of the ECHR were mentioned. Furthermore, the decision referred to Article 90 of the Constitution. Hence, it was defined that this could be applied in domestic law too. In other words, it was determined that the decisions of the ECHR and the provisions of the European Convention on Human Rights concerning freedom of religion and conscience can be evaluated within the context of conscientious objection, (Karaca 2012)

Although this case could be interpreted as a positive step, the judgement could be criticised in several ways. First, it requires one's affiliation with a group that refuses military service. The military court interpreted the ECtHR's case law as though it requires one to be only a member of a religious belief system. In other words, the military court showed a tendency to accept the refusal of military service only when it is based on the rejection of an 'intellectual, religious, or political group, as such' (Yildirim 2012). Therefore, it obliged conscientious objectors to be affiliated with any group that is opposed to military service. However, as indicated in *Kalac v. Turkey*, in which the applicant was exposed to forced retirement, 'religious freedom is primarily a matter of individual conscience'.[17] Second, the Court rejected Delice's claims on the grounds that he declared his objection after serving five months of military service. Thus, the court held that his motivations were not 'sole and undivided'. The Court evidently required conscientious objectors to declare their objection before they are conscripted and ignored the right to change one's beliefs.

In another case before the military court, the applicant, Aydemir, left the military during his term of service and did not return to his regiment because of religious beliefs forbidding him to serve the secular Republic of Turkey. Moreover, he stated that he could serve only in an army that derives its laws and principles from the Qur'an. The military court stated that under the ECHR, claiming the right to conscientious objection must be grounded on 'beliefs'.

Accordingly, individuals are required to be members of a belief system to exercise the right to conscientious objection. Idealist, political or any other personal reasons are inadequate. In other words, the right to conscientious objection is protected if it is based on an established belief system instead of an individual opinion. Thus, according to the Court, conscientious objection means refusing military service based on objectors' membership of a religious, political or intellectual group. The Court concluded that Aydemir's objection was not grounded on his religious beliefs but instead on idealist and political opinions; therefore, his claim could not be protected under the right to religion or belief. Furthermore, since he claimed that he could serve in another army ruled by another political regime, there was no serious and insurmountable conflict with his religious beliefs.[18]

In brief, as explained before, the Republic of Turkey's Constitution has flexible provisions enabling the implementation of exemption from military service. For instance, the Constitution protects the right to freedom of conscience, religion and belief and freedom of expression. However, the judiciary has been unwilling to implement these provisions when dealing with cases of conscientious objection. Claims regarding the recognition of conscientious objector status have not been considered in accordance with international human rights jurisprudence. Such claims are examined under the influence of a widespread understanding that prioritises protecting national security and maintaining the state's power over any other human rights (Yildirim 2010: 80). Even though the domestic courts recognise the right to freedom of thought, conscience and religion, they require those claiming the right to conscientious objection to be subscribed to a specific group. Furthermore, the domestic courts reject conscientious objectors' claims on the grounds that ethical and political objections are not protected under Article 9 of the ECHR. They adopt a restrictive approach and exclude ethical and political motivations from the scope of the right to conscientious objection. Their approach complies only with the international arena's traditional approach.

The Criminalisation of Conscientious Objection

The Ne Bis in Idem *Principle*

Those who decide to be objectors and refuse the militarist structure of society face the threat of punishment for the rest of their lives. The soldier's choice to be an objector whilst serving in the army leads to endless prosecutions under military rules (Yildirim 2010: 75). In the civilian sphere, objectors face prosecution under Article 318 of the Turkish Criminal Code, entitled 'alienating people from military service' for publicly declaring their objection. It is clear that objectors are under threat of being punished until they accept service in the army. As noted by the United Nations Working Group on Arbitrary Detention,

> conscientious objection – which has its theoretical basis in the freedom of conscience and thus of opinion – gives rise, particularly in countries that have not yet recognized conscientious objector status, to repeated criminal prosecutions followed by sentences of deprivation of liberty which are renewed again and again.[19]

Similarly, in concluding observations on the initial report of Turkey in 2012, the Human Rights Committee highlighted that since the right to conscientious objection has not been recognised, objectors and their supporters are still at risk of repeated prosecutions because of their persistent refusal to perform military service.[20] Such a persistent refusal also raises concerns over whether the second refusal can be considered a new act, subjecting the objector to another punishment. On this point, the Human Rights Committee, in its General Comment No. 32, stated that:

repeated punishment of conscientious objectors for not having obeyed a renewed order to serve in the military may amount to punishment for the same crime if such subsequent refusal is based on the same constant resolve grounded in reasons of conscience.[21]

The Working Group on Arbitrary Detention, in a communication concerning Osman Murat Ulke, also considered the question of whether, 'after an initial conviction, each subsequent refusal to participate in military service does constitute a new offence and gives rise to a fresh conviction'.[22] After he declared his objection, Ulke was detained and subjected to seven sentences of imprisonment. The Working Group concluded that:

since, after the initial conviction, the person exhibits, for reasons of conscience, a constant resolve not to obey the subsequent summons, [. . .] there is 'one and the same action entailing the same consequences and, therefore, the offence is the same and not a new one' [. . .] Systematically to interpret such a refusal as being perhaps provisional (selective) would, in a country where the rule of law prevails, be tantamount to compelling someone to change his mind for fear of being deprived of his liberty if not for life, at least until the date at which citizens cease to be liable to military service.[23]

In its *Ulke v. Turkey* opinion, the Working Group on Arbitrary Detention focused on whether imprisonment of the objector after the initial imprisonment was deemed arbitrary. In its opinion on *Halil Savda v. Turkey*, however, the Working Group examined whether the initial imprisonment of the objector was arbitrary:

On previous occasions, [the Working Group] has already declared arbitrary the detention of conscientious objectors following a second conviction on the grounds that this would be tantamount to compelling a person to change his or her convictions and beliefs for fear of not being subjected to criminal prosecution for the rest of one's life, being incompatible with the principle of double jeopardy or ne bis in idem, thus violating article 14, paragraph 7 of the ICCPR.[24]

As this passage illustrates, the Working Group once more considered the repeated convictions of objectors to be arbitrary. What is distinctive about this case is that the Working Group, this time, examined whether *the first* criminalisation of objection was arbitrary. Highlighting the fact that restrictions on the right to freedom of religion, belief and conscience are not justified, the Working Group decided that the applicant was a 'genuine conscientious objector and restrictions on the applicant's right to freedom of religion and belief are not justified'. Therefore, it maintained that Savda's convictions, *including the initial one*, were arbitrary.[25]

Since Turkey has not adopted any legislation that protects conscientious objectors from punishment, conscientious objectors are repeatedly accused of the same crime. However, international instruments now suggest that the right to conscientious objection stems from the right to freedom of conscience, thought and religion. Also, they ask states to amend any legislation that permits the repeated prosecution of objectors. Similarly, in its recommendation, the Working Group asks states that have not recognised the right to conscientious objection to grant objectors conscientious objector status. It further states that 'such prosecutions should not give rise to more than one conviction, so as to prevent the judicial system from being used to force conscientious objectors to change their convictions'.[26] Furthermore, the UN Commission on Human Rights emphasises that states should refrain from 'subjecting objectors to imprisonment and to repeated punishment for failure to perform military service'.[27] It also states that 'no one shall be liable or punished again for an offence for which he has already been finally convicted or acquitted'.[28]

The Right to Fair Trial

According to Article 14(1) of the ICCPR,[29] 'in the determination of any criminal charge against [them], or of [their] rights and obligations in a suit at law, everyone shall be entitled to a fair and public hearing by a competent, independent and impartial tribunal established by law'.[30] In its General Comment No. 32, the Human Rights Committee clearly notes that such requirements, enshrined in Article 14 of the ICCPR, apply to all courts, both civilian and military. While there is no provision in the Covenant prohibiting military courts from trying civilians, the Covenant requires military and special courts to comply with the rules laid down in Article 14 of the ICCPR. The nature of the court cannot be an excuse not to apply or to limit the requirements of Article 14. Therefore, courts are still bound by these rules. Since the trial of civilians in military courts might cause serious equity problems, it is vital to ascertain that these trials are held genuinely and with a full guarantee of the provisions enshrined in Article 14. Such trials, special and military, should be exceptional. The State Party also should show the 'objective and serious reasons' requiring states to resort to such trials.[31] The United Nations Human Rights Committee also declares that 'the requirement of competence, independence and impartiality of a tribunal [. . .] is an absolute right that is not subject to any exception'.[32] According to the Committee, states should protect judges from any political intervention to guarantee their independence. States should provide this protection through the constitution and domestic law, setting objective criteria and clear procedures around judges' obligations and rights.[33]

To explore whether Turkey complies with the right to fair trial in the case of conscientious objectors, it is worth analysing its domestic law, which in the past gave military courts the competence to try civilians. Before the 2010 amendment, Article 145 of the Constitution provided that:

> Military justice shall be dispensed by military courts and military disciplin-
> ary organs. These courts and tribunals shall be responsible for conducting
> proceedings concerning offences committed by military personnel, which
> are breaches of military law or are committed against other military per-
> sonnel, on military premises or in connection with military service and the
> related duties.
>
> Military courts shall also be responsible for dealing with *offences committed
> by civilians* where these are designated by special laws as breaches of mili-
> tary law, or have been committed against military personnel, either during
> their performance of duties designated by law or on military premises so
> designated.[34] (emphasis added)

The Turkish Constitution before the 2010 amendments explicitly recog-nised that military courts had the competence to try civilians for offences under military rules.[35] This has been the concern of the ECtHR. In the case of *Ergin v. Turkey*,[36] the applicant, following publication of an article entitled 'Giving the conscripts a send-off, and collective memory' (*Asker uğurlamalar ve toplumsal hafıza*), was accused of evading military service and, therefore, sentenced to imprisonment by the Military Court of the General Staff.[37] The European Court considered that, as a member of the Council of Europe, Turkey was the only country that explicitly and con-stitutionally gives military courts competence to try civilians in peace-time.[38] According to the Court, 'situations in which a military court has jurisdiction to try a civilian for acts against the armed forces may give rise to reasonable doubts about such a court's objective impartiality'.[39] In this regard, the Court concluded that:

> it is understandable that the applicant, a civilian standing trial before a court
> composed exclusively of military officers, charged with offences relating to
> propaganda against military service, should have been apprehensive about
> appearing before judges belonging to the army, which could be identified

with a party to the proceedings. Accordingly, the applicant could legitimately fear that the General Staff Court might allow itself to be unduly influenced by partial considerations. The applicant's doubts about the independence and impartiality of that court can, therefore, be regarded as objectively justified.[40]

In the case of *Ercep v. Turkey*,[41] the applicant, a Jehovah's Witness, was regarded as a deserter because he failed to report for duty when he was called for military service. He was, therefore, sentenced to imprisonment by the military court. Since his first call-up, he consistently refused to do his military service. He faced further criminal proceedings until 2006,[42] when he was tried in a military tribunal. In this regard, the applicant alleged that 'as a civilian, to appear before a court made up exclusively of military officers' violates his right to fair trial. The Court considered that although he was subject to the Military Criminal Code, 'for criminal-law purposes' the applicant was still a civilian. The European Court further recalled domestic legislation in which the Turkish court decided that 'one can be regarded to be a member of the armed forces only from the time he or she reported for duty with regiment'.[43] Considering the applicant's circumstances, the European Court concluded that the applicant, 'as a civilian standing trial before the Court', had justifiable reasons to question the objectivity of a court ruled by judges from the army. As the army could be seen as a party to the proceedings, there was a risk that the military court might be influenced by partial considerations. The European Court also acknowledged that 'the applicant's doubts about the independence and impartiality of that court [are] objectively justified', and there was a violation of Article 6(1) of the Convention.[44]

The European Court also scrutinised the trials of civilians by military courts during peacetime in the case of *Düzgoren v. Turkey*,[45] in which the applicant was accused of 'inciting others to evade military service' because of distributing a leaflet on conscientious objection.[46] As a civilian tried in military court, the applicant alleged that the General Staff Court could not be considered independent and impartial. In this regard, he highlighted that the members of the Court are subject to 'the orders and instructions of the Military Defence'.[47] Considering whether a civilian could be tried in a military court, the European Court referred to its *Ergin v. Turkey* decision and once more decided that the trial of civilians by military courts is a violation of Article 6 of the ECHR.[48]

It is vital to emphasise that Turkey amended Article 145 in 2010, and following this amendment, military courts no longer have the competence to try civilians. The amended Article provided that:

military justice shall be exercised by military courts and military disciplinary courts. These courts shall have jurisdiction to try military offences committed by military personnel and offences committed by military personnel against military personnel or related to military services and duties. Cases regarding crimes against the security of the State, constitutional order, and its functioning shall be heard before the civil courts in any case. Non-military persons shall not be tried in military courts, except during a state of war.[49]

'Civil Death' of the Objectors

'They granted me two days to be enlisted and then released me in the recruiting office. It means the time of "civil death" started for me.'

(Mehmet Tarhan, conscientious objector)[50]

As a result of the non-recognition of the right to conscientious objection at the domestic level, when they refuse to become part of the military's hierarchical structure, objectors face human rights violations. They run the risk of prosecutions and convictions. After serving their sentence, they are asked to join the army, which leads objectors to make new declarations that are seen as new acts that should be punished. In addition to the risk of repeated punishments, conscientious objectors also face additional and unequal treatment because of their refusal, such as losing the chance to find a job and the right to pursue a parliamentary seat (or even vote) because the law allows only those who have performed their military service to be elected as members of parliament. This is how 'civil death' starts for them. According to a report published by the Association for Conscientious Objection, between January and April 2021 thirty-six conscientious objectors contacted the Association regarding the human rights violations that they face in their daily lives. Restrictions on conscientious objectors' freedom of movement were amongst the most frequently stated human rights violations.[51] The report also reveals that objectors' freedom of movement is restricted, mostly because of regular identity checks during domestic travel, at passport control points or when checking in at hotels. These identity checks disclose a person's military service status and force them to declare their objection one more time, which automatically exposes them to new fines and prosecutions. In addition to their right to free movement, objectors also mostly stated that their right to work is violated because they can neither work in public institutions nor find a job with social security. According to Article 48 of the Civil Servants' Act No. 657, to be employed as a civil servant a person needs not to be affiliated with the military or not to be of military age; if he has reached the age of military service, he must have done or postponed his regular military service. In addition, under the Military Penal Code employers also risk prosecution if they employ draft evaders (Yıldırım and Üçpınar 2021).

The Contradiction Between Article 318 of the Turkish Criminal Code and Article 10 of the ECHR

Decker and Fresa (2000: 379) define conscientious objection as a 'manifestation of freedom of conscience, i.e. freedom to think and act according to one's own conscience, as well as freedom not to be psychologically forced in the formation and the declaration of one's thoughts'. This definition illustrates that the right to freedom of expression is vital to exercising the right to conscientious objection. Conscientious objectors and their supporters, as they criticise the government's policy on military matters, need protection against arbitrary detention and the risk of prosecution so as to be able to declare the motivations behind their refusal, convince the decision-making bodies or raise public awareness on matters that go against their beliefs and thoughts. Activities pertaining to public matters, such as peaceful demonstrations and activists' public speeches, must be protected to allow members of society to enter into free public debates. Interferences with non-violent activities that aim at raising awareness on public matters in most cases[52] violate Article 10 of the Convention (Voorhoof and Cannie 2010: 413). Criminalising support for the conscientious objector, which has mostly resulted in the closure of non-governmental organisations that support antiwar activities, contravenes Article 10 of the Convention, which reads as follows:

1. Everyone has the right to freedom of expression. This right shall include freedom to hold opinions and to receive and impart information and ideas without interference by public authority and regardless of frontiers. This Article shall not prevent States from requiring the licensing of broadcasting, television or cinema enterprises.
2. The exercise of these freedoms, since it carries with it duties and responsibilities, may be subject to such formalities, conditions, restrictions or penalties as are prescribed by law and are necessary in a democratic society, in the interests of national security, territorial integrity or public safety, for the prevention of disorder or crime, for the protection of health or morals, for the protection of the reputation or rights of others, for preventing the disclosure of information received in confidence, or for maintaining the authority and impartiality of the judiciary.[53]

Although the right to manifest religion and belief is protected under Article 9(2) of the Convention, the right to freedom of expression intersects with the right to religion, thought and conscience, particularly in situations that involve declaring objections to military service and criticising the use of force. This makes Article 10 of the Convention relevant to conscientious objection cases. Conscientious objectors' declarations mostly criticise sensitive issues, such as the government's right to go to war and maintain national security. As such, declarations could lead to prosecutions in some legal frameworks (as in Turkey), and to gain protection against arbitrary detentions, conscientious objectors and their supporters need full enjoyment of their right to freedom of expression.

It is well established that the right to freedom of expression is qualified, and there are certain restrictions on its implementations.[54] One of the main aims of these restriction clauses is to prevent 'the irresponsible and dangerous use of democracy' (Flauss 2009: 810). In this sense, restrictions on enjoyment of the right are not limitless. Any restrictions on the freedom of expression must be compatible with the 'triple test' of Article 10(2) of the Convention. Therefore, restrictions must 'have a legitimate aim', be 'prescribed by law' and be 'necessary in a democratic society'. Unlike Article 9(2), Article 10(2) considers national security a legitimate ground for restricting the right to freedom of expression. The complexity of the right to freedom of expression mostly reveals itself in the conflict between protecting national security and enabling free speech (Campbell Public Affairs Institute 2003: 4–5).

In most cases of freedom of expression and national security in Turkey, the European Court held that 'although the language used had a hostile tone and described the Turkish population in a negative way, it did not constitute incitement to violence'.[55] In two conscientious objection cases, *Savda v. Turkey* and *Ergin v. Turkey*, the European Court interpreted Article 10(2) in a restricted manner. In *Savda v. Turkey*, the applicant was convicted and sentenced by the Istanbul Criminal Court of First Instance to five months' imprisonment under Article 318 of the Turkish Penal Code for alienating people from military service.[56] Although the applicant claimed that the criminal sanctions against him violated Articles 9 and 10 of the Convention, the European Court examined his claims under Article 10 only.[57] In the present case, following the European Court's request, the Turkish state provided the Court with information on how the Turkish domestic courts apply Article 318 of the Criminal Code. The information provided suggests that, first, the Istanbul Criminal Court of First Instance acquitted the applicant in May 2013 on the grounds that although his statements contained strong criticism, they were not directed at inciting violence. Unless they encourage the public to revolt or soldiers to desert, these statements are protected under Article 26 of the Turkish Constitution and Article 10 of the ECHR. Second, in December 2012, Eskişehir Criminal Court of First Instance relied on both domestic and international human rights referred to in Article 26 of the Turkish Constitution, Article 10 of the ECHR, and Articles 18 and 19 of the Declaration of Human Rights. It held that Savda's statements were within the ambit of freedom of expression; therefore, there was no violation of Article 318. In December 2012, Eskişehir Criminal Court of First Instance considered Savda's statements to fall within the ambit of freedom of expression as they did not incite violence. Third, Istanbul Üsküdar Criminal Court of First Instance held in March 2011 that the nature of Savda's statement, which was deemed to be 'wrong, disturbing, uneasy, extreme, oppositional', and his views, which contradicted those of the majority, were insufficient to find him guilty. Fourth, contrary to these decisions, Nusaybin Criminal Court of First Instance convicted Savda in March 2011 under Article 318 of the Criminal Code.[58]

In the present case, although the European Court appreciated the Turkish Courts' interpretation of Article 318 of the Turkish Penal Code in the light of Article 10 of the ECHR,[59] the Court once again stated that Turkey's domestic law is inadequate to solving problems pertaining to a refusal to serve in the army on the grounds of belief.[60] The Court also indicated that alienating people from military service itself does not constitute a legitimate ground for restricting the right to freedom of expression. Although the statements involve hostile views towards military service, they do not incite violence, hate and revolt.[61] Therefore, restrictions on the right to freedom of expression are not necessary for a democratic society;[62] consequently, Article 10 was violated.[63]

In the *Ergin v. Turkey* case,[64] Ergin was charged under Article 155 of the Criminal Code (current 318 of the Penal Code) in 1997.[65] According to the military court,

> military service was a constitutional duty and . . . the applicant, by denigrating military service, had also denigrated the struggle against the PKK, a terrorist organization which killed soldiers, police officers, teachers and civil servants. It held that the offending article contained terms contrary to morality and public order.

In a similar vein, the government indicated that:

> the applicant's conviction was necessary in a democratic society because the article was offensive to the wounded and the families of conscripts who had

been killed during their military service, and that the criticisms of military service were contrary to morality and the public interest.[66]

According to the European Court, the article's wording, even though hostile and offensive, did not incite violence nor amount to hate speech.[67] Also, unlike the case of *Arrowsmith v. the United Kingdom*, in which the applicant distributed a leaflet to encourage soldiers to desert, the applicant's statement in the present case was published in a public newspaper and 'did not seek, either in its form or in its content, to precipitate immediate desertion'.[68] Therefore, restrictions on the applicant's freedom of expression breached Article 10 of the Convention.[69]

Limitations on human rights based on the maintenance of national security have thus been the concern of European Court case law, in which the Court establishes certain criteria under the 'quality of law test'. Accordingly, the test requires the 'laws to be foreseeable, that they should restrain the discretion of those to whom they confer powers, and that safeguards should be created to guard against the abuse of such powers' (Leigh and Born 2008: 52–3). The Johannesburg Principles[70] were also adopted in 1995 to clarify the legitimate grounds for restricting free speech: namely, national security. Given the complexity of restricting the right to free speech to protect national security, these principles set basic standards for the protection of freedom of expression (Campbell Public Affairs Institute 2003: 1). Similarly, as noted above, limitations on free speech must meet the triple-test criteria[71] of the Convention. The simple consideration of the issue as a national security matter by the state does not restrict freedom of expression (Article 19 and Liberty 2000: 1–2). As stated in Principle 4(b) of the Tshwane Principles, 'it is not sufficient for a public authority simply to assert that there is a risk of harm; the authority is under a duty to provide specific, substantive reasons to support its assertions'.[72]

The level of respect for democracy and human rights differs among members of the European Council despite such international principles and criteria. Given these differences, the effectiveness of Article 10 on the implementation of the right to freedom of expression varies (Voorhof 2009: 19). Further, there is a clear danger of abuse of power by states. As pointed out by Laurence Lustgarten and Ian Leigh (1994: 20–1), the authorities are in a position that enables them to restrain any criticism and public debates on their policy. Authorities also appeal to national security as an excuse for their lack of respect for democracy. Highlighting the danger of abusing the national security concept, they consider the use of national security in the political arena 'as a sort of intellectual curare, inducing instant paralysis of thought'. Accordingly, given their 'extraordinary power'

in the name of securing freedoms, the security agencies themselves constitute a significant danger of 'destroying those freedoms, and even democracy itself' (Lustgarten and Leigh 1994: 363). Similarly, Thomas Scanlon
argues that 'freedom of expression becomes controversial when expression
appears to threaten important individual interests [. . .] or to threaten some
important national interest such as the ability to raise an army' (Scanlon
2003: 519). The national security concept is mainly appealed to when justifying restrictions on speeches directed at criticising the government's policy
on public matters, such as those pertaining to the environment, government decisions in waging war, and so on (Coliver 1999: 12–13). Article
318 of the Turkish Criminal Code constitutes one of the best examples
of this situation. The criminalisation of supporters, particularly journalists
and human rights activists, under Article 318 of the Turkish Criminal Code
violates their right to freedom of expression. It aims to silence any dissent
and reduces the arenas where individuals can raise their concerns regarding
a public matter. However, the right to freedom of expression is one of the
fundamental rights found at both international and regional levels, and
the right is protected in various instruments. For instance, Article 10(1)
of the ECHR states that 'this right shall include freedom to hold opinions
and to receive and impart information and ideas without interference'.[73]
Similarly, ICCPR Article 19(2) protects individuals' freedom 'to seek,
receive and impart information and ideas of all kinds'.[74] Mine Yıldırım
(2010: 88) also draws attention to the fact that freedom of expression is
protected under Article 19 of the ICCPR and Article 10 of the ECHR in a
way that also covers the 'freedom to have opinions and freedom to receive
and impart information'. Accordingly, individuals adopting the belief that
killing is wrong have the right to disseminate their ideas and receive any
information about their convictions. However, conscientious objectors
are under the threat of being punished for declaring their motivations in
public under Article 318 of the Turkish Criminal Code. Before the 2013
amendment, the Turkish Criminal Code Article 318 stated that:

1. Persons who give incentives or make suggestions or spread propaganda
   which will have the effect of discouraging people from performing military service shall be sentenced to imprisonment for a term of six months
   to two years.
2. If the act is committed through the medium of the press and media, the
   penalty shall be increased by half.[75]

With the fourth judicial package passed into law by Parliament, paragraph 1 of Article 318 now provides that 'people who urge those

carrying out their military service to desert or suggest to those who are yet to carry out their military service to be dissuaded from carrying it out are imprisoned for six months to two years'.[76] Although the new version of the Article refers to 'dissuading' people from performing military service instead of 'alienating' people from military service, Article 318 of the Turkish Criminal Code, as stated by objector Halil Savda (2010), is still 'the armour of militarism'. The Article would continue to put objectors at risk of prosecution for their declaration.

Furthermore, as noted by Üçpınar (2009: 248), although objectors have been prosecuted under Article 318 of the Turkish Criminal Code, the Article is also applied to prosecute journalists and human rights defenders who make and publish supportive declarations of objectors.[77] Thereby, Article 318 is intended to prevent any claim or public discussion on the right to conscientious objection. Similarly, while drawing attention to the aggravation clause of Article 318, which states that 'if the act is committed through the medium of the press and media, the penalty shall be increased by half',[78] the Organization for Security and Cooperation in Europe (OSCE) Representative on Freedom of the Media clearly noted that 'with Article 318 on Discouraging people from performing military service, it in fact becomes punishable for journalists to report or debate on the military service' (Haraszti 2005: 4). Thomas Hammarberg, Commissioner for Human Rights of the Council of Europe, following his visit to Turkey in 2011, also noted that the Turkish Penal Code – namely, Article 318 – allows criminal proceedings against journalists and human rights defenders, which give rise to violations of the right to freedom of expression.[79] He also states that:

> as regards cases concerning convictions for having published statements which were considered to incite abstention from compulsory military service, six judgments of the Court against Turkey await execution. Pursuant to Article 318 of the Criminal Code, the non-violent expression of opinions on conscientious objection is still a criminal offence [. . .] He [The Commissioner] has been informed that in June 2010 four persons were sentenced by an Ankara court to imprisonment ranging from 6 to 18 months for having issued a press release in favour of a conscientious objector, Enver Aydemir.[80]

Conclusion

The national legislation on compulsory military service in Turkey reveals that states' response to international bodies' tendency towards recognition of the right to conscientious objection shows considerable variety and involves contradictions not only with the international standards but also within the domestic legal system. For example, as indicated by Üçpınar (2009: 244), 'the constitution explicitly recognizes freedom of conscience while the law explicitly criminalizes the exercise of this constitutional freedom'. As a result of this contradiction and the fact that the right to conscientious objection is not recognised, objectors have faced a number of convictions. First, since there is no specific provision in Turkish law on the right to conscientious objection, objectors run the risk of facing a series of criminal convictions, which might subject them to inhuman and degrading treatment. Second, objectors and their supporters are deprived of their right to freedom of expression based on Article 318 of the Turkish Criminal Code, which penalises both objectors and their supporters. At this point, Turkey needs legislation that protects objectors from 'civil death'. The principle of *ne bis in idem* should be applied. Furthermore, Article 318 of the Turkish Criminal Code considers any criticism of the military as a potential threat to the military's integrity. The right to freedom of expression, which is a fundamental principle of a democratic society, is ignored. Any public declaration might be regarded as alienating people from military service. Thus, criticising the militarist structure of society and behaving according to one's conscience become a challenging task.

Notes

1. The effect of the international treaties at the domestic level is worthy of analysis in order to establish whether Turkey complies with international standards on the right to fair trial. Article 90 of the Turkish Constitution provides thus: 'International agreements duly put into effect have the force of law. No appeal to the Constitutional Court shall be made with regard to these agreements, on the grounds that they are unconstitutional [. . .] In the case of a conflict between international agreements, duly put into effect, concerning fundamental rights and freedoms and the laws due to differences in provisions on the same matter, the provisions of international agreements shall prevail.' Furthermore, according to Article 27 of the Vienna Convention on the Law of Treaties, 'a party may not invoke the provisions of its internal law as justification for its failure to perform a treaty'.
2. Constitution of the Republic of Turkey Act No. 2709, Article 72.
3. Law on Military Service Act No. 1111, 20 March 1927, Article 1.
4. Unlike Article 45 of the Military Criminal Code, the Turkish Constitution protects the right to religion and conscience. Article 24, entitled 'Freedom of Religion and Conscience', stipulates that 'everyone has the right to freedom of conscience, religious belief and conviction', and Article 25, entitled 'Freedom of Thought and Opinion', rules that 'everyone has the right to freedom of thought and opinion.

No one shall be compelled to reveal his[her] thoughts and opinions for any reason or purpose, nor shall anyone be blamed or accused on account of his[her] thoughts and opinions' (see 1982 Constitution of the Republic of Turkey Act No. 2709, 7 November 1982).

5. Military Criminal Code Act No. 1632, 22 May 1930, Article 45.
6. Constitution of the Republic of Turkey Act No. 2709, Article 76.
7. UN Human Rights Committee, Concluding observations on the initial report of Turkey adopted by the Committee at its 106th session (15 October to 2 November), CCPR/C/TUR/CO/1 para.23. available at: https://tbinternet.ohchr. org/_layouts/15/treatybodyexternal/TBSearch.aspx?Lang=En&CountryID=179 &ctl00_PlaceHolderMain_radResultsGridChangePage=6 [accessed 19 January 2022].
8. Article 67 of the Turkish Constitution, entitled 'right to vote, to be elected and to engage in political activity', reads as follows: 'in conformity with the conditions set forth in the law, citizens have the right to vote, to be elected, to engage in political activities independently or in a political party, and to take part in a referendum'.
9. 1982 Constitution of the Republic of Turkey Act No. 2709, Article 11.
10. Article 10 of the Turkish Constitution states that 'everyone is equal before the law without distinction as to language, race, colour, sex, political opinion, philosophical belief, religion and sect, or any such grounds [. . .] No privilege shall be granted to any individual, family, group or class.'
11. Enver Aydemir, Eskisehir Military Court Case No. 2013/164 Decision No. 2013/349 (5 July 2013).
12. Muhammed Serdar Delice, Malatya Military Court, Case No. 2012/98 Decree No. 2012/40 (24 February 2012).
13. Enver Aydemir, Eskisehir Military Court, Case No. 2013/164 Decree No. 2013/349 (5 July 2013).
14. Parliamentary Assembly of the Council of Europe, Resolution 337(1967), January 26, 1967.
15. Muhammed Serdar Delice, Malatya Military Court, Case No. 2012/98 Decree No. 2012/40 (24 February 2012).
16. The Court referred to the *Bayatyan*, case in which the Court stated that the applicant in the present case was a member of the Jehovah's Witnesses, a religious group whose beliefs include the conviction that service, even unarmed, within the military is to be opposed. The Court, therefore, had no reason to doubt that the applicant's objection to military service was motivated by his religious beliefs, which were genuinely held and were in serious and insurmountable conflict with his obligation to perform military service.
17. *Kalac v. Turkey* App. No. 20704/92 (ECtHR, 1 July 1997) at para.27.
18. Enver Aydemir, Eskisehir Military Court, Case No. 2013/164 Decree No. 2013/349 (05 July 2013).
19. Working Group on Arbitrary Detention, United Nations, 'Recommendation 2: Detention of Conscientious Objectors E/CN.4/2001/14' para.91.

20. UN Human Rights Committee, Concluding observations on the initial report of Turkey adopted by the Committee at its 106th session (15 October to 2 November), CCPR/C/TUR/CO/1 para.23. available at: https://tbinternet.ohchr.org/_layouts/15/treatybodyexternal/TBSearch.aspx?Lang=En&CountryID=179&ctl00_PlaceHolderMain_radResultsGridChangePage=6 [accessed 19 January 2022].

21. UN Human Rights Committee (HRC), General comment no. 32, Article 14, Right to equality before courts and tribunals and to fair trial, 23 August 2007, CCPR/C/GC/32, para.55 available at: https://www.refworld.org/docid/478b2b2f2.html [accessed 19 January 2022].

22. United Nations Working Group on Arbitrary Detention, 'Civil and Political Rights, Including Questions of Torture and Detention Opinion No. 36/1999 (9 November 2000) E/CN.4/2001/14/Add.1' para.8. Available at: <https://digitallibrary.un.org/record/431623?ln=en#record-files-collapse-header> (last accessed 19 January 2022).

23. Ibid. at para.9.

24. United Nation Working Group on Arbitrary Detention, Promotion and Protection of All Human Rights, Civil, Political, Economic, Social and Cultural Rights, Including the Right to Development Opinion No. 16/2008 (Turkey), 9 May 2008, A/HRC/10/21/Add.1, para.39. available at: https://documents-dds-ny.un.org/doc/UNDOC/GEN/G09/107/13/PDF/G0910713.pdf?OpenElement [accessed 19 January 2022].

25. Ibid. at para.38.

26. United Nation Working Group on Arbitrary Detention, Recommendation 2: Detention of Conscientious Objectors, E/CN.4/2001/14, para.94.

27. UN Commission on Human Rights, Conscientious objection to military service, 22 April 1998, E/CN.4/RES/1998/77, available at: https://www.refworld.org/docid/3b00f0be10.html [accessed 21 January 2022].

28. Ibid.

29. In a similar vein, Article 6(1) of the ECHR provides this: 'in the determination of his civil rights and obligations or of any criminal charge against him, everyone is entitled to a fair and public hearing within a reasonable time by an independent and impartial tribunal established by law'.

30. International Covenant on Civil and Political Rights, 19 December 1966, Article 14.

31. UN Human Rights Committee (HRC), General comment no. 32, Article 14, Right to equality before courts and tribunals and to fair trial, 23 August 2007, CCPR/C/GC/32, para.22 available at: https://www.refworld.org/docid/478b2b2f2.html [accessed 19 January 2022].

32. Ibid. at para.19.

33. Ibid.

34. The 1982 Constitution of the Republic of Turkey, Article 145.

35. As amended on 12 September 2010, Act No. 5982 Article 145 provides this: 'military justice shall be exercised by military courts and military disciplinary courts. These courts shall have jurisdiction to try military offences committed by

military personnel and offences committed by military personnel against military personnel or related to military services and duties. Cases regarding crimes against the security of the State, constitutional order and its functioning shall be heard before the civil courts in any case. *Non-military persons shall not be tried in military courts*, except during a state of war' (emphasis added).

36. *Ergin v. Turkey* App. No. 47533/00 (ECtHR, 4 May 2006).
37. Ibid. at para.7.
38. Ibid. at para.21.
39. Ibid. at para.49.
40. Ibid. at para.54.
41. *Ercep v. Turkey* App. No. 43965/04 (ECtHR, 22 November 2011).
42. In 2006, the Parliament passed a new law under which military courts no longer had jurisdiction to try civilians.
43. *Ercep v. Turkey* App. No. 43965/04 (ECtHR, Press Release 254(2011).
44. Ibid.
45. *Duzgoren v. Turkey* App. No. 56827/00 (ECtHR, 9 November 2006).
46. Ibid. at para.8.
47. Ibid. at para.16.
48. Ibid. at para.22.
49. The 1982 Constitution of the Republic of Turkey amended Article 145.
50. See <https://bianet.org/english/people/167724-conscientious-objector-tarhan-released-facing-civil-death> (last accessed 5 January 2022).
51. 'I couldn't vote (5); I was fired from my job (7); My freedom of travel was restricted (20); My freedom of education was denied (5); My bank accounts were confiscated (2); I cannot get a job with social security (28); I have been prosecuted more than once because of the same action (6); I cannot work in the state sector (19).'
52. See *Acik and Others v. Turkey* App. No. 31451/03 (ECtHR, 13 January 2009).
53. European Convention on Human Rights, 3 September 1953, Article 10.
54. It is worth clarifying that the limitations on the right to freedom of expression in military issues have a wide range of effects on both military personnel, who criticise the conditions of service in the military, and civilians, who criticise the military and the government's policy on military matters. In this regard, military discipline and maintenance of national security might constitute legitimate limitations on free speech (Leigh and Born 2008: 58). However, freedom of expression for members of the armed forces will not feature in this book and the focus will remain on restrictions of civilian critiques of the military. For a soldier's critique of the military, see *Engel and Others v. the Netherlands* App. Nos. 5100/71; 5101/71; 5102/71; 5354/72; 5370/72 (ECtHR, 8 June 1976).
55. *Okcuoglu v. Turkey* App. No. 24246/94 (ECtHR, 8 July 1999) at [48]; see also *Incal v. Turkey* App. No. 41/1997/825/1031 (ECtHR, 9 June 1998); *Surek and Ozdemir v. Turkey* App. Nos. 23927/94, 24277/94 (ECtHR, 8 July 1999).
56. Savda v Turkey App. No. 2458/2 (ECtHR, 15 November 2016) para. 8.
57. Ibid. at para.15.

58. Ibid. at para.14.
59. Ibid. at para.24.
60. Ibid. at para.20.
61. Ibid. at para.26.
62. Ibid. at para.29.
63. Ibid. at para.30.
64. *Ergin v. Turkey* App. No. 47533/99 (ECtHR, 4 May 2006).
65. Ergin's statement went as follows: 'This last week in bus stations has been a time for sending the August conscripts on their way . . . The novice soldiers setting off – "but you'll soon be back", people tell them to console them – already seemed during these ritual send-offs to be plunging into war by donning "invisible khaki". It was a time when war seemed rather attractive; the congratulations and praises made it seem like a warm nest, almost as warm as a mother's arms, into whose embrace they would have liked to run. What we saw at each of these ceremonies shows that the thing has become a collective hysteria and that this hysteria has also spawned its own indispensable attributes: the traditional drum and clarinet, the famous three-crescented flag, sometimes accompanied by the corn-ear flag of the RP [Welfare Party] or the rose-bearing flag of the BBP [Great Union Party] . . . Warm-up ceremonies are organised for those setting off for the war, the exaltation felt on killing a man is the exaltation of winning a match and, what is more, the killer justifies his act by speaking of the love he has for his fatherland and his nation. In short, it can't be said that what we're doing is right . . . Those verses, written by a fallen soldier, are carved on his own tombstone. He will no longer see those who gather to give the conscripts a send-off, no longer hear the drum, the clarinet or the gunfire, not be able to read the verses written on his tombstone, on seeing which he would perhaps have felt repelled by the determinism they convey. Because from now on he is reduced to a title: a martyr . . . It is because the State does not recognise as such the war which is etched deeply into the collective life and the collective memory that, apart from a small minority, those who return from it after losing an arm, a leg or an eye receive no allowance. These people who are no longer capable of meeting their own needs are being deceived by talk of fictitious jobs. There is a war, but not officially; you are war-wounded, but you count for nothing' (Ibid. at para.11).
66. Ibid. at para.29.
67. Ibid. at para.34.
68. Ibid.
69. Ibid. at para.35.
70. For instance, Principle 2.b states that: 'In particular, a restriction sought to be justified on the ground of national security is not legitimate if its genuine purpose or demonstrable effect is to protect interests unrelated to national security, including, for example, to protect a government from embarrassment or exposure of wrongdoing, or to conceal information about the functioning of its public institutions, or to entrench a particular ideology, or to suppress industrial unrest.' The Johannesburg Principles on National Security, Freedom of Expression and Access to Information, 1 October 1995' para.2.b. Available at: <http://www.refworld.

org/docid/4653fa1f2.html> (last accessed 28 September 2017). Furthermore, Tshwane Principle 2.b also states that: 'Given that national security is one of the weightiest public grounds for restricting information, when public authorities assert other public grounds for restricting access – including international relations, public order, public health and safety, law enforcement, future provision of free and open advice, effective policy formulation, and economic interests of the state – they must at least meet the standards for imposing restrictions on the right of access to information set forth in these Principles as relevant.' The Global Principles on National Security and the Right to Information: The Tshwane Principles para 2.b. Available at: <https://www.justiceinitiative.org/uploads/bd50b729-d427-4fbb-8da2-1943ef2a3423/global-principles-national-security-10232013.pdf> (last accessed 28 September 2017).

71. Principle 3 of the Tshwane Principles reads as follows: 'No restriction on the right to information on national security grounds may be imposed unless the government can demonstrate that: (1) the restriction (a) is prescribed by law and (b) is necessary in a democratic society (c) to protect a legitimate national security interest; and (2) the law provides for adequate safeguards against abuse, including prompt, full, accessible, and effective scrutiny of the validity of the restriction by an independent oversight authority and full review by the courts.'

72. The Global Principles on National Security and the Right to Information: The Tshwane Principles: 12 June 2013. (Open Society Foundations 2013) para.4.b.

73. European Convention on Human Rights, 3 September 1953, Article 10.

74. International Covenant on Civil and Political Rights, 19 December 1966, Article 19(2).

75. The new Turkish Criminal Code No. 5237, 26 September 2004, Article 318.

76. The new Turkish Criminal Code Amended Law No. 5237, 26 September 2004, Article 318.

77. See, for example, the following news reports: 'Conscientious Objector Mustafa Karayay Acquitted in Ankara Court' (IFEX). Available at: <http://www.ifex.org/turkey/2009/04/16/conscientious_objector_mustafa/> (last accessed 30 August 2017); 'Four Rights Activists on Trial for "Alienating the Public against the Military"' (IFEX). Available at: <https://ifex.org/four-rights-activists-on-trial-for-alienating-the-public-against-the-military/> (last accessed 30 August 2017); 'Two Women Journalists Critical of Militarism Targeted by Nationalist Newspaper' (IFEX). Available at: <http://www.ifex.org/turkey/2008/01/22/two_women_journalists_critical/> (last accessed 30 August 2017); 'Writer on Trial for Supporting Conscientious Objector; Several Others Await Verdicts in Climate of Courtroom Violence' (IFEX). Available at: <http://www.ifex.org/turkey/2006/06/05/writer_on_trial_for_supporting/> (last accessed 30 August 2017).

78. The new Turkish Criminal Code No. 5237, 26 September 2004, Article 318.

79. United Nations Commissioner for Human Rights, 'Report by Thomas Hammarberg, Commissioner for Human Rights of the Council of Europe Following His Visit to Turkey, from 27 to 29 April 2011: Freedom of Expression and Media Freedom in Turkey' para.16.

80. Ibid. at para.19.

CHAPTER 4

A Typology of Conscientious Objection in Turkey

A commitment to share the benefits and burdens of political life in some equitable fashion – the (occasional) the need to kill is surely the most awful of the burdens.

(Walzer 1970: 121)

Introduction

The backgrounds of conscientious objectors and the circumstances which led them to question the normalisation of militarisation show a considerable variety. The motivations behind their non-conformity with the law also differ. This makes it difficult to come to a unified definition because people attribute different meanings to conscientious objection and base their objection on various philosophical, moral, political or religious beliefs. Conscientious objection is defined in its general sense as 'refusal to participate in the armed services based upon opposition to war. This opposition may rest upon reasons of religious belief, philosophy, morality or political ideology' (Lippman 1990: 31). The term 'conscientious objector' generally refers to 'a person who refuses either to bear arms or to serve in the military or continue to serve in the military because of religious or moral beliefs that are opposed to killing, or, more recently, are opposed to relying on nuclear weapons for deterrence' (Moskos and Chambers 1993c: 5). These definitions focus only on non-participation in the army. They do not capture the critique of militarism that is embodied in the act of refusal. This chapter seeks a broader understanding of conscientious objection. It follows Moskos and Chambers's (1993a) typology of conscientious objection: first, private or political objection; second, universalist or selective objection; and third, alternativist or absolutist objection. It examines various motivations behind the act of conscientious objection and addresses the question of whether – in addition to religious motivations – 'moral, ethical, humanitarian, or similar convictions' constitute legitimate grounds for asserting the right to conscientious objection (Major 2001: 5).

The Nature of Conscientious Objection to Military Service in Turkey[1]

Conscientious objectors might be secularly (private or political objection) or religiously motivated (Moskos and Chambers 1993c: 5). Whereas moral and ethical convictions are accepted as sources of objection in some states, religious motivations might be the only recognised source of objection to serving in the military in other states (Marcus 1997: 539). Historically, conscientious objectors initially refused military service because of their religious belief. In the sixteenth century, members of Protestant churches, including Quakers, grounded their objection on the Sixth Commandment, which forbids individuals from killing: 'Thou shalt not kill' (Zürcher 2009: 45). The early religious objectors' main argument in refusing secular laws rested on the idea that they should obey only the laws of God (Bröckling 2009: 54). Indeed, religious beliefs were at this time the most common ground used for asserting the right to conscientious objection. In this context, while some states required objectors to be affiliated with a specific church, such as peace churches, others extended the scope of protection to include any religious belief that condemned war (Lippman 1990: 37). Although the new approach, which recognises objection based on any religious grounds even if objectors are not pacifist, is more inclusive, it still refuses to accept non-religious grounds for objection (Marcus 1997: 540).

During the 1960s and 1970s, the conscientious objection movement gained a new momentum. International efforts to protect human rights and individual dissent against dominant institutions led to the emergence of a new type of conscientious objection. The scope of conscientious objection has, therefore, expanded to include a wide range of motives that are not limited to religious beliefs (Moskos and Chambers 1993a: 201). In fact, conscientious objection embraces different forms of beliefs that are not constrained by a particular religion. The United Nations Commission on Human Rights also states that 'conscientious objection to military service derives from principles and reasons of conscience, including profound convictions, arising from religious, moral, ethical, humanitarian or similar motives'.[2] In a similar vein, 'belief' does not necessarily refer to a religious belief; it can also be non-religious, according to United Nations documents (Lerner 2006: 7). For instance, United Nations Special Rapporteur Arcot Krishnaswami indicates that both of the terms 'religion' and 'belief' cover 'agnosticism, free thought, atheism and rationalism' (quoted in Lerner 2006: 7). Belief is an umbrella term that includes religion in its non-traditional meaning (Lerner 2006: 7). Black's Law Dictionary defines belief as 'a conviction of truth of a proposition, existing subjectively in the mind, and induced by argument, persuasion, or proof addressed to the judgement'.[3] This definition captures the various sources of belief. Within this formula, how individuals make sense of their existence and interpret events is embedded in their belief system, a system which is not restricted to religious beliefs.

In the interviews I conducted, the richness of belief systems is well captured by *Mehmet Lütfü Özdemir*. *Mehmet* is an essay writer and a novelist, who expresses himself in three different ways: as an anarchist, a revolutionist and a *tevhidi*. He explains *tevhid* and his religious stand as 'seeing humans – with no discrimination of colour, race, religion and sex – animals, trees, the universe, and the environment as equivalent to each other'. He also explains his religious view as 'a desire to achieve heaven on earth with no class, exploitation and war'. Even though *Mehmet* was a religious conscientious objector, his focus was shifting to the conscientious, political and cultural aspects of his religious stance. He states that 'religion is a way of life. It means the way you go. Which way am I going? I am taking a path without class, exploitation, war . . . I am trying.' He considers his objection as religious and political, and that it leads him to take this direction:

> Neoliberal policies are imposed, shopping centres are constructed [everywhere], they have transformed us into a consumer-oriented society . . . My conscience must differ from this point of view [. . .] They took culture, love, art away from us. They are building a new way of life and asking us to shape our lives from their perspectives. Actually, that's what we reject. We tell them that 'this is not us'.

Indeed, the link between political activism and conscience was one of the recurring themes that emerged during the interviews. For instance, *Ercan Jan Aktaş* expresses himself as an oppositional and an anarchist. He is a columnist and activist working on war, resistance and conscientious objection. He is also a member of a working group focusing on war, trauma and confrontation issues. He considers his consciously informed decision to be the result of his political identity: 'Since we aim to be politically consistent and act in accordance with our political views, objecting is the honourable thing to do.' *Burak Özgüler*, an animal rights activist, veterinarian and anarchist, states that

> this is something we can't do: wearing a uniform, killing someone or an animal, burning the forest. I don't think it would change much if they imprison us [. . .] My rejection is also a political stance because my conscience does not allow me to do so [*vicdanım bunu kaldırmıyor*].

Burak's statement reveals that objecting to serve in the army and freedom of conscience are two sides of the same coin. Conscience allows individuals to think, evaluate, observe and act in accordance with their own values. Individuals' right to self-determination is also closely related to freedom of conscience. It gives people the opportunity to develop and manifest their understanding of what is right or wrong. It is an expression of the individual's uniqueness – personal identity (Decker and Fresa 2000: 379). Therefore, limiting the right to conscientious objection to religious beliefs only, first, poses a challenge to conscientious objectors whose aim, in the case of a clash between their conscience and state needs, is to enjoy their right to freedom of thought, conscience and belief. Second, it 'neglects the human ability to form personal opinions and interpret their espoused religion in an individualized way' (Marcus 1997: 540).

Conscientious objectors consider compulsory military service as a burden on their conscience that they cannot carry. As Michael Walzer indicates, 'a commitment to share the benefits and burdens of political life in some equitable fashion – the (occasional) the need to kill is surely the most awful of the burdens' (Walzer 1970: 121). Recognising that compulsory military service is a burden on the conscience of those condemning killing raises the question of why protecting conscience is deemed to be important. The answer is straightforward: a conscientiously motivated act is seen as 'an individual's inward conviction of what is morally right and morally wrong, and it is a conviction that is genuinely reached and held after some process of thinking about the subject' (quoted in Wolff 1982: 67). In this regard, conscience occupies a special place in the thinking of those who prioritise their own definition of what is right and wrong over the state's. When someone adopts the belief that killing is morally wrong, performing compulsory military service, which requires people to bear arms against 'enemies', clashes with such a conscientiously held belief. The link between compulsory military service and conscience is also articulated as follows: 'the moral revulsion of the convinced conscientious objector at the thought of taking human life is great. Military conscription of such men necessarily entails grave interference with conscience' (quoted in Wolff 1982: 68). Similarly, it is argued that

> the conscience of the individual is a precious asset for every society. It is part of the socialization process to nurture and encourage the moral conscience of the individual, without which civilization would be meaningless. At the centre of this process is the effort to instil in the individual the conviction that it is immoral in most circumstances to take the life of other persons. Some exceptions to this moral principle are widely recognized, however, including the right to use force in self-defence when no other option seems possible. But it is also widely held that no one should deliberately place [themselves] in a position in which [they] will find it necessary to defend [themselves].[4]

Universal Refusal of Compulsory Military Service

The second classification of objection is grounded on the extent to which objectors oppose serving in the army. In this context, objection might be universalistic or selective (Moskos and Chambers 1993c: 5). While universalistic objectors oppose all kinds of conflicts based on their pacifist view that killing is always wrong, selective objectors refuse to participate in particular wars rather than refusing war in general (Marcus 1997: 541). Selective conscientious objectors evaluate the morality of the specific war in which they are asked to participate. They base their refusal on the distinction between wars that are 'proper arenas for their participation and other wars that [. . . are] morally bad' (Griggs 1979: 93). The main difference between selective objectors and absolutists is the scope of their refusal. Whereas selective objectors distinguish between different kinds of military participation and have more specific motivations, absolutists refuse all sorts of military action (Lubell 2002: 410). Generally, selective objectors base their objection on the illegality of using force. Hence, the most prominent ground for their rejection is the concept of a just war, which requires a just cause to wage war (justification for waging war: *ius ad bellum*) and waging this war justly (conduct of war: *ius in bello*) (Lubell 2002: 417). When they base their objection on the just war theory, selective objectors take into consideration whether waging war is the last resort and whether the war is fought justly and proportionally (Clifford 2011: 23).

The necessity of including selective conscientious objection within the scope of the legal recognition of conscientious objection can be explained in two ways. First, as it is stated,

> the ultimate test of a free society is the extent to which individuals are able to carve out their own destiny on the basis of reflective choice. In shaping one's destiny, a few [sic] options are more fundamental than the choice between killing and not killing. (Kaufman 1968: 262)

Conscription systems put people, even those who conditionally accept the idea of waging war, in a morally and physically sensitive position (Coady 1997: 385). That is to say, war embraces deeply moral issues, such as killing other human beings or taking part in an act that might result in depriving people of their basic needs. As a result, it requires serious thinking even by those who agree to be part of war. Within this framework, the recognition of selective objection means giving those who offer conditional support to states' war efforts the freedom to decide whether they can bear the consequences of their participation in the war after evaluating its cause and means, and also their moral boundaries.

Second, although selective conscientious objection is mostly a manifestation of a belief forbidding people from participating in specific wars, such as those involving the use of illegal weapons (Hammer 2002: 164), selective objection is not necessarily based on the declaration of an inner belief. Political motivations such as asking for a change in national policy, particularly in the defence area, might constitute a ground for selective refusal. In this case, the right to selective objection, followed by a political statement criticising the government's political decisions over engaging in a particular war, can be derived from the right to freedom of expression. As indicated by Leonard Hammer, 'motivation is a matter of personal stimulation, where the individual is provided with an incentive for conducting an action. Such an incentive can be derived from a belief, but not in any necessary manner' (Hammer 2002: 166). Therefore, selective objectors should be able to express their concerns even if they are not objecting to military service in general but only to specific wars. In other words, 'considering that the importance of a conscientious belief is not merely its existence but also its application to specific instances, the application also should entail instances of selective conscientious objection' (Hammer 2002: 168).

The right to selective objection is mostly neglected. Mention of selective objection, either prior to or after conscription, can hardly be found in international and domestic regulations (Clifford 2011: 22). For state authorities, the recognition of the right to selective conscientious objection poses a threat against their right to wage wars when required and to compel citizens to participate in the war effort. Furthermore, granting selective objectors a status on the grounds that individuals question their government's policy endangers the state's ability to maintain its security (Coady 1997: 386). Since they refuse all actions involving the use of force, whatever the political circumstances may be, absolute objectors do not pose a significant threat to the state's authority compared to selective objectors (Lubell 2002: 412). On the contrary, selective objectors question the state's current political decisions in engaging in particular military actions. Hence, this refusal is directed at the state's authority to resort to specific military actions. In this context, their refusal can be easily considered as a political threat (Lubell 2002: 412–13).

Selective conscientious objectors also face great difficulties compared to alternativists (see below) in terms of proving their sincerity. While alternativists are required to prove that they will carry a gun and join the military under no circumstances whatsoever, selective objectors are obliged to convince the authorities of their motivations, which depend on specific circumstances and differ over time. To assess the underlying motivations forbidding individuals to fight, the decision-makers, for instance, are likely to ask objectors whether they would take up arms and defend their beloved family in the case of real and immediate danger. In that case, while absolutists' self-defence claim is acceptable, it is not obvious whether the positive answer of selective objectors means that they are insincere (Lubell 2002: 413–14).

As stated before, the right to selective conscientious objection is neglected in the international arena. There is a lack of explicit legal recognition of selective objection. The only reference to selective objection can be found in the United Nations General Assembly's Resolution 33/165 (Lubell 2002: 411), which 'recognizes the right of all persons to refuse service in military or police forces which are used to enforce apartheid'.[5] Similarly, the 1985 report to the Sub-Commission states that 'objection to military service may also be partial, related to the purposes of or means used in armed action' (Asbjern and Chama 1985: para.19). Although these documents do not specifically and explicitly recognise selective objection, they recommend the recognition of selective objection in cases of gross human rights violations, such as apartheid and genocide (Lubell 2002: 411). Furthermore, the Human Rights Committee's General Comment No. 22 states that

> the Covenant does not explicitly refer to a right to conscientious objection, but the Committee believes that such a right can be derived from article 18,

inasmuch as the obligation to use lethal force may seriously conflict with the freedom of conscience and the right to manifest one's religion or belief.[6]

This can be interpreted to mean that the Human Rights Committee's General Comment on Article 18 recognises the selective conscientious objector's status based on their refusal to use lethal force. As indicated by Hammer (2002: 164–5), 'the term "lethal" can include selective objections to particular lethal weapons, such as using chemical weapons in warfare, even though the same person might not object to handling a gun or participating in the military, in contrast to a pacifist'.

Recognition of the right to selective conscientious objection is vital for individuals to maintain their moral values and act in accordance with them to improve their personal integrity. Compulsory military service puts individuals in a position that requires them to act contrary to their moral beliefs. When soldiers encounter situations forcing them to determine whether their conscience allows them to be part of such situations, and they do not have the right to 'say no', they are forced to act in a way that they consider immoral. On the contrary, recognising the right to selective objection gives some room for soldiers to engage in debate, and this reduces the risk of waging immoral wars. In this case, granting the right to selective objection, which is the moral responsibility of states, is an important step towards allowing selective objectors to raise their concerns over the morality of war (Clifford 2011: 32–5).

Conscientious objectors in Turkey can be classified as universal as all interviewees focused on the political nature of their refusal. The most frequently repeated motivation amongst the objectors that I interviewed was 'we will not serve in the current political situation, which promotes a war environment in Turkey'. For instance, having focused on the moral and philosophical reasons behind his act, *Halil Savda*, a Kurdish conscientious objector and a key public figure among objectors, identifies himself as a pacifist and an antimilitarist. He is the only objector to call himself a pacifist amongst those I interviewed. He summarises his objection with reference to his political view, saying:

My objection is moral because military service is a system based on killing human beings, and I believe that killing people is an immoral act. My objection is philosophical because I am an antimilitarist. I believe in non-violence, I believe in demilitarisation, and I believe in the necessary removal of all guns from our life. My objection is also political because there is a war environment. Politically, I do not want to be part of this war.

In a similar vein, *Muhammed Cihad Ebrari (Saatçioğlu)*, an activist and a researcher into Middle East studies and politics, who identifies himself as a peace and environmental activist, considers the current political situation as the main reason for his objection. But he also links his religious belief with his political stance. He says that

> I do not consider myself as a free person; in my opinion, we are all slaves who perform compulsory things against our will. We have an identity, a job and money. But I will never ever have a gun. Although military service is compulsory, it is still something that I can avoid. I have thousands of answers to the question of why I am objecting just as I have to the question of why I oppose the system. However, the most prominent one is that I will not serve such a government in these circumstances (even if it was a democratic one, I would not serve). To clarify, the current government pursues an imperialist policy in the Middle East and applies violence against Kurds, in which I would never take part. I adopt a belief which contradicts the current religionists. My belief is not cultural. It has impacts on my political stand. Therefore, my objection is both political and religious.

Ebrari highlights several times that he 'will never *become* a soldier'. This was a recurring theme among objectors: a direct rejection of the myth that 'every Turk is born a soldier'. It is also a reflection of the belief that 'soldiers are not born; rather they are made, through training, institutional expectations, psychological conditioning, and a variety of material and ideological rewards' (Whitworth 2004: 86). *Ercan* also relates his objection to his political views and explains his motivations as follows: 'my objection is political. I define my objection as an act that articulates my world-view; in a sense, it is individualistic. At the same time, it strengthens my political stand. Although being an objector is personal, it overlaps with my political views.'

Halil's, *Ercan's* and *Ebrari's* standpoints indicate the political aspects of conscientious objection. Moral and religious views lead to political confrontations, as a form of conscientious objection, with the government. In line with that, while explaining their political stance, the majority of objectors also focused on the hierarchical structure of the army. The common view amongst them was that 'we reject hierarchy for political and moral reasons'. For instance, *Bülent Bektaş*, a theatre actor, highlights his family's Alevi background. He thinks that Alevi beliefs have influenced his life, though he grew up in a secular family. He mentions that:

> My objection is political. As an anarchist, my reference point is to avoid being associated with the government and anything that is related to the

government. I organise my social circle in accordance with my political views. I would like to be in a place where there is no hierarchy – superior-subordinate relationship – and institutionalised violence, a place that is not full of guns and violence. In this respect, my objection is political and at the same time sociological and humanitarian.

While forging a link between the motivations behind his objection and his political stance, *Burak* adopts a different perspective. As a veterinarian, he objects on the grounds that war has an impact not only on people, but also on nature and animals. Accordingly, he explains the motivations behind his objection as follows:

My objection is political, conscientious and moral. I do not differentiate between them. I am an animal rights activist. In the Roboski massacre, hinnies were killed too. In my declaration, I focused on the effects of war on nature, animals and wildlife. My objection is the product of a long period of questioning government policies. However, I also morally and conscientiously refuse to serve. Wearing uniform, killing human beings, destroying a forest and killing animals are things most of us cannot do. Even if we were going to be put in prison, I do not think this will change anything.

Burak's animal rights activism and his narrative, which led him to confront the government's policies and refuse to serve in the army, demonstrate that objection in Turkey is not only moral and personal, but also political. That is to say, objectors turn their individual stories and what makes them uncomfortable into a political struggle.

Gökhan is a law student. He says with a laugh,

I am an LLM student but this has nothing to do with military service.[7] Our friend, Davut [Erkan], always says that Turkey's most intellectual people are conscientious objectors because in order to avoid or postpone their service, they keep registering in universities.

Gökhan introduces himself as an anarchist. However, he says that 'I am a conscientious objector not because I am an anarchist. I am an anarchist because I am an objector.' He summarises this viewpoint by reference to Tolstoy:

My objection is moral. As Tolstoy says 'everyone thinks of changing the world, but no one thinks of changing themselves'. Following this motto, I started to think of changing myself. Conscientious objection was a possible way to start. Also, as a lawyer, realising the injustice we face in a given situation in which we are right makes an impact on my objection.

Except for one objector, *Özge Günönü*,[8] a student who identifies herself as an anarchist, all women objectors also classified their objection as political, regardless of the fact that their main motivations are grounded on their anarchist, anti-authoritarian or feminist world-view. *Meltem Nur Tuncer*, a social care specialist, refuses to identify herself with any political views or any form of ethnicity, yet works with the Ankara Anarchist Initiative as it opposes all kinds of oppression. She states that

> my objection has a political meaning, which stems from a humanistic understanding. I can classify my objection in various ways. It rejects a wide range of issues. The common denominator of these rejections is my political stand. Although I am against all kind of militaries, the political situation in Turkey speeded up my objection.

Similarly, *Zeynep Çicek*, a sociologist, declared her objection on International Women's Day. She repeatedly, more than any other interviewee, identifies herself as a feminist and antimilitarist, and considers her objection as a political act that refuses gender roles.

Conscientious objectors in Turkey appear to have their own unique childhood stories leading them to adopt an antimilitarist perspective. The motivations behind their act vary to a great extent, yet the political nature of their motivations remains at the centre of their objection.

Absolute Refusal of Compulsory Military Service

The third classification of conscientious objection is based on the extent to which objectors agree to cooperate with the system. In this respect, objectors can be absolutists – who refuse to be part of the system, whatever the nature of the alternative service – or alternativists – who accept the performance of an alternative civil service in substitution for their military service (Moskos and Chambers 1993c: 5). The alternative civilian service can be considered as an opportunity for conscientious objectors to fulfil their national duties. Furthermore, the alternative service might be seen as necessary 'to balance the individual's interest in exemption from military service against the state's interest in ensuring that the individual contribute to the national defense and welfare' (Lippman 1990: 39). In other words, alternativists are willing to serve in any substitute service which is civil in nature. Their willingness to accept such service might seem to be an indication that they are not escaping from a duty and that they are 'sincere' (Moskos and Chambers 1993c: 5). For instance, in its decision in N v. Sweden, the European Commission considered the national authorities' restrictions on exempting total objectors as 'understandable' on the grounds that the purpose of the alternative service reduces the risk of 'insincere claims' used to 'escape' military service.[9]

Alternative civilian service might be a solution for those who object to joining the army – based on internal convictions forbidding the taking up of weapons – as opposed to those refusing to be part of any militarist structure. Yet, the recognition of conscientious objection with an alternative civilian service raises concerns – even for those who agree to perform civilian service – over administrative issues, such as the duration, the type and the nature of the alternative service and the consequences of disobeying such an alternative service (Noone 1993: 187). At the international and regional levels, human rights protection bodies such as the Council of Europe Parliamentary Assembly and Commission on Human Rights issued a number of recommendations and comments setting fundamental rules on the nature of the alternative service. For instance, the Parliamentary Assembly recommends that states adopt 'genuine alternative service of a clearly civilian nature, which should be neither deterrent nor punitive in character'.[10] Similarly, the Committee of Ministers, in Recommendation R (87) 8,[11] sets rules on the alternative civilian service. Accordingly, 'alternative service shall not be of a punitive nature'.[12] Furthermore, 'conscientious objectors performing alternative service shall not have less [sic] social and financial rights than persons performing military service'.[13] The United Nations High Commissioner also

> reminds states with a system of compulsory military service, where such provision has not already been made, [. . .] that they provide for conscientious objectors various forms of alternative service which are compatible with the reasons for conscientious objection, of a non-combatant or civilian character, in the public interest and not of a punitive nature.[14]

It should be noted that despite the wide range of resolutions and recommendations on an alternative civilian service, each country approaches this service in a different way.[15] Implementation of the alternative service varies from one state to another, depending on the degree of importance attached to national security and the balance between protection of national service and an individual's freedom of religion, thought and conscience. For example, the alternative service is seen in some cases as a punishment rather than a right, particularly when 'it consists in hard work without a meaningful content' (Eide and Chama 1985: para.152). When the application of the alternative service at the national level is incompatible with these basic standards, conscientious objectors continually face repeated punishments because of their persistent refusal. Furthermore, alternative service also constitutes a problem for total objectors, who refuse to be a part of the military in any way. Objectors who refuse civil service because they consider it as part of military service face the risk of repeated prosecution (Lippman 1990: 39).

Exemption from military service mostly entails alternative service within conscription systems. However, in Turkey, not all conscientious objectors accept the alternative service because their objections are grounded in different motivations. While some objectors are willing to accept non-combatant duty within military service, such as medical or administrative tasks, others might oppose taking any part in the military.[16] During the interviews, some of the participants were sceptical about alternative civilian service yet open to negotiation. *Ebrari*, for instance, says: 'If there is a civil social service and they pay a salary, I will accept it. If we think about what we are doing now, we are the gears of this wheel anyway.' In the case of *Abuzer Yurtsever*, who identifies himself as leftist because of his Kurdish identity, his understanding of an alternative civil service is no different from *Ebrari*'s. He states that 'If it is a civilian duty, I will evaluate it according to its conditions. I can agree to work as a civilian in the state institution.' *Muhammed Serdar Delice*'s reason for accepting the alternative civil service differs completely from that of *Ebrari* and *Abuzer*. *Serdar*, who owns his own company, expresses himself as a Turk and a nationalist. However, he refuses to be identified as a member of the Nationalist Party. He clearly does not want to be associated with either the opposition parties or those in power (*iktidar*). He explains his acceptance of alternative civil service as follows:

I definitely support alternative civil service. We must show people our patriotism. The [whole] world is my homeland. Being a patriot does not mean to say, 'I would die for the homeland.' I would support and encourage alternative civil service in order to show that service to homeland is not restricted to holding a gun.

When conscientious objection is not recognised as having a legal status, objectors' declarations on non-participation in military service give rise to human rights violations, particularly to repeated prosecutions that may cause the 'civil death' of objectors.[17] In this respect, it is important to bear in mind the question of whether recognition of conscientious objection with an alternative service could put an end to repeated prosecutions of conscientious objectors. Indeed, an alternative civilian service might be a solution to repeated prosecutions of alternativist conscientious objectors because rejection of military service based on fundamental values forbidding individuals from taking another human being's life does not always mean rejection of all social responsibilities. The rejection might pertain only to the use of violence and the killing of other human beings in certain circumstances. In these circumstances, conscientious objectors are not necessarily refusing their national duty in any manner. Therefore, they might be willing to serve in different ways that do not require them to use violence (Lippman 1990: 36). Parallel to these observations, some of the interviewees, even though they explained that they would still reject the performance of an alternative service, acknowledged that civilian service might be a solution, particularly for deserters or some conscientious objectors who limit their objection to refusing the taking up of guns, killing or dying in a war. *Oğuz Sönmez*, an activist and an expert on conscientious objection, indicates that

> There are millions of deserters in Turkey. If such a law is introduced, 90 per cent, maybe 99 per cent, will try to benefit from this law. Some of the conscientious objectors will also do so. But for total objectors, antimilitarists and anarchists, this would not be enough. Compulsory military service is an imposition [*dayatma*], and civil service is also an imposition. It is not possible to accept this.

Davut Erkan, consultant with the Association of Conscientious Objection and lawyer for objectors, identifies himself as an anarchist. Instead of making a public declaration, *Davut* announced his objection before the Constitutional Court. In fact, he was the first conscientious objector to have lodged an individual complaint with the Court. He says that

> If alternative service arrives, a large number will benefit from it, but I think a large majority of those who declare their refusal will say 'No'. Most total objectors, even though they don't specifically use the term 'total',[18] declare in their statements that they will not take part in authoritarian organisations. In this sense, when we take these statements into consideration, I think that the vast majority of conscientious objectors will also refuse the alternative service. Such a service indirectly feeds the army and war. I think that if conscientious objection is recognised as a right and alternative service is provided, the movement will evolve into total refusal.[19]

Interviewees highlighted the hierarchical structure of the army. Perceiving his objection as 'only one piece of a whole', *Bülent* refuses to 'submit [himself] to someone else's will'. *Ercan* also says, 'compulsory military service itself is a chore, I will not be subject to it, but I will not be subject to its alternative either.' *Gökhan* also believes that alternative service is 'a compulsion from the state. Alternative service must also be voluntary.' As has been seen, an alternative civilian service might cause additional problems for absolutists who refuse to be involved in any kind of alternative services, even if they are civilian in nature, thus refusing to be part of the state authority through the conscription system (Moskos and Chambers 1993c: 5).

Despite the fact that male conscientious objectors had various views about alternative civil service, all women conscientious objectors clearly refused any alternative service, no matter whether it is civil or not.[20] Almost all women conscientious objectors used the term 'system'. For them, their objection is directed at refusing the 'system'. For *Atlas Arslan*, women 'refuse at all costs because [they] do not want to serve this system'. *Zeynep* believes that 'this is not just a process of holding a gun, dying and killing. It is also the rejection of any institution that is geared towards the creation and continuation of war.' *Didem Doğan*, an English teacher, similarly rejects the alternative civil service: 'my refusal was a refusal to serve the *system*, and I will stand against it whenever I need to serve the system'.

It seems, then, that an alternative service raises additional problems for absolutists, who refuse to be part of the military in any way. The traditional approach to conscientious objection assumes that religious conscientious objectors would accept alternative services. Accordingly, insofar as they are not asked to use weapons, they might agree to performing an alternative service. This approach ignores the fact that conscientious objectors in peacetime may refuse to be part of the armed forces, whatever the type of service they are requested to perform. Therefore, many conscientious objectors in such a case will also reject the alternative service, even when it is civil in nature (Noone 1993: 186).

Conclusion

Conscientious objection challenges the state's authority to enlist soldiers and questions the militarist structure of society (Marcus 1997: 512); it rejects what is considered the most basic duty of individuals – defending their country. As a result, it has enormous impacts on the individuals' position vis-à-vis their states (Moskos and Chambers 1993c: 3).

Ercan captures such conflict by referring to the reaction of his family and extended social circle to his objection. He states that:

> My family was aware that my political identity would lead me to select my own path, and that they would have no say about it. Getting used to the idea was not an easy task for them. The uncertainty of my situation, of course, causes physiological problems for those close to me like my mother or my partner. When the social circle extends, you face reactions. For example, my extended family members uphold the opinion that 'you have been in this situation for ten years; you should have done your military service by now!' The problem gets bigger when this circle extends to the societal level. It is not a family matter any more; you enter into conflict with society. Because you are born as a Turk in Turkey, it does not matter which ethnicity your family comes from. The motto 'every man is born a soldier' prevails. Being a soldier is an exalted duty. Manliness involves certain responsibilities, such as getting married and being the head of the family. All of these are related to military service. If you reject serving in the army, you are not a first-class citizen. In these circumstances, you are in conflict with both the requirements of being a citizen and social expectations.

The objectors' narratives and their motivations suggest that conscientious objection in Turkey has both moral and political grounds. Their objection has social and legal implications that subject them to 'civil death'. In that sense, the majority of objectors to military service are not private objectors.[21] It is not just the inner feeling of individuals against wars. Objectors cooperate with other people objecting to the militarist construction of society. The aim of objectors is not only to refuse military service but to bring about social, political and legal change. They express their objection publicly and try to raise awareness of militarist and gendered structures in society.

Notes

1. In this chapter, the narratives of the male conscientious objectors will override those of the female objectors (see Chapter 6 for women's objection).
2. UN Commission on Human Rights, Conscientious objection to military service, 22 April 1998, E/CN.4/RES/1998/77, available at: https://www.refworld.org/docid/3b00f0be10.html [accessed 19 January 2022].
3. *Black's Law Dictionary*, 6th edn (1990: 155), cited in Lerner (2006: 7).
4. United Nations, Conscientious Objection to Military Service, 1985, E/CN.4/Sub.2/1983/30/Rev.1, para.22 available at: https://www.refworld.org/docid/5107cd132.html [accessed 19 January 2022].

5. United Nations General Assembly, 'Status of Persons Refusing Service in Military or Police Forces Used to Enforce Apartheid, 20 December 1978, A/RES/33/165'. Available at: <http://www.refworld.org/docid/3b00f1ae28.html> (last accessed 14 April 2017).

6. United Nations Human Rights Committee, 'CCPR General Comment No. 22: Article 18 (Freedom of Thought, Conscience or Religion), 30 July 1993, CCPR/C/21/Rev.1/Add.4', para.11. Available at: <http://www.refworld.org/docid/453883fb22.html> (accessed 14 April 2017).

7. In Turkey, students are allowed to postpone military service till the age of thirty. To avoid compulsory service, men usually enrol on MA courses.

8. Özge's classification of her objection differs from that of other objectors. She explains, 'I am an anarchist. My objection is also conscientiously motivated. In fact, the current circumstances in the region, the war environment, governmentality (erk zihniyeti) and the fact that how governments and power interfere in our life with oppression are the main factors contributing to the rise of my objection. My objection is not grounded on religious or ethnic motivations. I refused the military because I am a human and an anarchist. Anarchism is a lifestyle. I do not want to devalue my objection by calling it political.'

9. N v. Sweden App. No. 10410/83 (ECtHR, 11 October 1984).

10. Council of Europe: Parliamentary Assembly, 'Recommendation 1518 (2001): Exercise of the Right of Conscientious Objection to Military Service in Council of Europe Member States' para.5.iv. Available at: <http://www.refworld.org/docid/5107cf8f2.html> (last accessed 14 April 2017).

11. Council of Europe: Committee of Ministers, 'Recommendation No. R (87) 8 of the Committee of Ministers to Member States Regarding Conscientious Objection to Compulsory Military Service'. Available at: <http://www.refworld.org/docid/5069778e2.html> (last accessed 14 April 2017).

12. Ibid. at para.10.

13. Council of Europe: Committee of Ministers, 'Recommendation No. R (87) 8 of the Committee of Ministers to Member States Regarding Conscientious Objection to Compulsory Military Service' para.11. Available at: <http://www.refworld.org/docid/5069778e2.html> (last accessed 14 April 2017).

14. UN Commission on Human Rights, Conscientious objection to military service, 22 April 1998, E/CN.4/RES/1998/77, para.4 available at: https://www.refworld.org/docid/3b00f0be10.html [accessed 19 January 2022].

15. For instance, in Armenia, the Alternative Service Act entered into force in July 2004. Section 3.1 says: 'An Armenian citizen whose creed or religious beliefs do not allow him to carry out military service in a military unit, including the carrying, keeping, maintenance and use of arms, may perform alternative service.' And 'Alternative service includes the following types: (a) alternative military [service, namely] military service performed in the armed forces of Armenia which does not involve being on combat duty or the carrying, keeping, maintenance and use of arms; and (b) alternative labour [service, namely] labour service performed outside the armed forces of Armenia.' Despite the recognition of a

Law on Alternative Service, there is no improvement in the situation of conscientious objectors at a national level. Objectors are still required to perform their so-called civilian service, which requires a twenty-four-hour presence under the strict control of the military; any demand regarding a change of task is subject to military confirmation; they have the same identification card as individuals undertaking military tasks; they are required to wear uniform, which makes them part of the Armenian military forces; and the length of the alternative service is double. It is clear that in these circumstances, alternativist conscientious objectors cannot perform alternative service, as it is not genuine (Muzny 2012: 145–6).

16. United Nations and Office of the High Commissioner, *Conscientious Objection to Military Service* (2012) at 65. Available at: <https://www.ohchr.org/Documents/Publications/ConscientiousObjection_en.pdf> (last accessed 20 January 2021).

17. During the interviews, objectors avoided talking about this issue. While some of them specifically requested 'please do not depict us as vulnerable', others mentioned only briefly that they had stopped staying in hotels and driving on specific roads to avoid identity checks by the police. Since they mostly preferred to talk about their motivations for bringing about change in our militarised daily lives, I refrained from asking them questions on 'civil death' and left it for them to decide whether they wanted to elaborate on it.

18. For example, *Atlas*, without being asked, mentioned this point: 'I have not underlined total rejection [in my declaration], but this is an essential element of the conscientious objection of each of us. I do not accept alternative service.'

19. In the case of *N v. Sweden*, the applicant states, in the letter explaining his reasons for not complying with the law, that 'the non-armed service of today is a substitute for military service. To accept non-armed service thus implies acceptance of the principle of liability to military service. I do not accept that the State has any "right" to draft me or others for education in the technique of mass murder.' *N v. Sweden* App. No. 10410/83 (ECtHR, 11 October 1984).

20. Another major difference between male and female conscientious objection was that although the majority of the male conscientious objectors that I interviewed problematise masculinity, gender awareness was not considered as the *main* motivation behind their act. Most female conscientious objectors considered the hidden impacts of militarism on people, with a particular focus on women's life as the main motivation behind their act (see Chapter 6).

21. Private objectors do not try to convince others about their motivations; therefore, their objection cannot be considered as an act of civil disobedience.

CHAPTER 5

Conscientious Objection as an Act of Civil Disobedience

> The conscientious objector is a revolutionary. On deciding to disobey the law [s]he sacrifices [her]his personal interests to the most important cause of working for the betterment of society.
>
> (Einstein 2010: 257)

Introduction

The conflict between conscience and law puts individuals in a position to determine whether their conscience allows them to obey or disobey the law (Allan 1996: 103). When they morally decide to disobey orders, dissenters do not aim to destroy the legal system. Their act of civil disobedience is a 'way of manoeuvring between these conflicting moralities' (Walzer 1970: 24). Dissenters base their acts on the grounds that political circumstances clash with their deepest moral convictions. Therefore, the act of disobedience naturally involves conscientious grounds (Bedau 1961: 659). Such commonality, the fact that acts of both conscientious objection and civil disobedience encapsulate conscientious foundations, raises questions over the determination of the rights and duties of individuals. To what extent conscientious disobedience can be tolerated is also debated (Brownlee 2012: 4). Furthermore, to date no agreement has been reached over whether violence eliminates the civility of acts or whether the authorities should distinguish between ordinary criminals and law-breakers with a conscientious reason. As a result of these disagreements, it is hard to come to a comprehensive definition of civil disobedience; therefore, its scope remains ambiguous (Bedau 1991: 49).

In an attempt to clarify the differences and similarities between conscientious objection and the act of civil disobedience, one can draw on

Rawls's definition of civil disobedience and conscientious refusal[1] as a point of departure. In *A Theory of Justice*, Rawls (1999: 320) defines civil disobedience 'as a public, non-violent, conscientious yet political act contrary to law usually done with the aim of bringing about a change in the law or policies of the government'. He further points out that '[b]y acting in this way one addresses the sense of justice of the majority of the community and declares that in one's considered opinion the principles of social cooperation among free and equal men [sic] are not being respected' (Rawls 1999: 320). Each civil disobedience element suggested by Rawls raises concerns over the definition and scope of civil disobedience. However, before examining these elements in depth, it is important to analyse Rawls's focus on 'the sense of justice of the majority'.

Rawls's reference to 'the sense of justice of the majority of the community' has been criticised in that it restricts the legitimisation of disobedience. According to Peter Singer (1991: 124–6), although Rawls does not suggest that the sense of justice is a common denominator among societies, he mainly focuses on those having 'a common conception of justice'. In that sense, Rawls's understanding of the justification for civil disobedience is narrow. One should question why disobedience is acceptable only if directed at a 'particular conception of justice' and why it has to be based on already established societal principles. Rawls has a narrow understanding of civil disobedience because he excludes claims that are not intended to invoke the 'majority's shared conception of justice'. However, in some specific cases, disobedience may aim at invoking and obtaining the support of the minority. For instance, vegetarians, who believe that, as defenceless beings, animals deserve protection, usually attempt to gain the support of the minority. If Rawls's elements for justifiable disobedience were applied, acts of dissent aimed at gaining the support of a small community rather than the majority would not be qualified as disobedient civil acts (Greenawalt 1991: 176–7). Robin Celikates (2016: 985) also rejects Rawls's requirement for invoking the 'majority's sense of justice'. She highlights that it is the majority's sense of justice that actually impels individuals to disobey. The disobedient act aims at restoring the majority's distorted understanding of justice. Mahatma Gandhi or Martin Luther King would not invoke civil disobedience if the majority already empathised with them.

Rawls identifies four civil disobedience elements: first, civil disobedience is a non-violent act; second, dissenters are willing to accept punishment; third, civil disobedience is a public act; and fourth, civil disobedience is an illegal act. This chapter discusses these elements in turn and engages with the current philosophical debate on civil disobedience by providing empirical evidence of the differences and the similarities between civil disobedience and conscientious objection in Turkey. Drawing on the motivations behind conscientious objectors' acts of refusal, it explores the political roots of objection by considering the difference between a personal and a political act and forging a link between civil disobedience and conscientious objection.

Conscientious Objection is an Act of Civil Disobedience Because . . .

Objectors' Rejection is Non-violent . . . . But Must a Civil Disobedience Act be Non-violent?

According to Rawls (1999: 321–2), since the act of civil disobedience has conscientious implications, resorting to violence will be contrary to the basic sense of civil disobedience. Furthermore, the non-violent act of disobedience is an indicator that dissenters respect the law, though they disobey it. That is to say, using coercive tools which intimidate and threaten others and force them to behave against their rights and liberties is not compatible with the act of civil disobedience. Therefore, to achieve their sincere aim of bringing about a change in policies or laws, dissenters must consider negotiating and finding common ground rather than imposing their truth on policymakers (Brownlee 2004: 347). Parallel to this, all the interviewees I met referred to the non-violent nature of the objectors' act. The act itself is indeed a rejection of war and violence. *Gökhan* indicates that 'objectors refuse on moral and political grounds, a legal obligation by non-violent means. Since the act itself aims at refusing guns, it draws on public speeches and declarations. It is done to transform society.' However, objectors were also concerned about differentiating between being a pacifist, an antimilitarist and, more specifically, an objector. Their understanding of civil disobedience does not necessitate excluding violence and *any* coercion from its definition. This was clear from *Ebrari*'s statements. While talking about violence, he refers to the distinction between violence against himself as an individual and violence against groups. He stresses that 'If there is violence against me, I hold on and do not engage in violence as long as I can, but if we are a group or a movement and we are attacked, then we have the right to retaliate proportionately.'

Civil disobedience would become ineffective if the political structure were to limit disobedience to engaging in a 'purely symbolic protest'. To be able to make real impacts on society, political struggles mostly demand 'real confrontations', such as 'blockades or occupations' (Celikates 2016: 988). Further, in some cases, harms caused by non-violent acts might be more serious than the consequences of violent acts. Therefore, violence cannot be completely excluded from the concept of civil disobedience (Raz 1979: 267). Furthermore, individuals do not merely have *prima facie* rights over their bodies. They are also free to make up their own mind. Therefore, any acts that physically or physiologically restrict the autonomy of individuals in deciding freely are also considered as acts of violence. As a result, it becomes difficult to argue that civil disobedience does not involve violence (Morreall 1991: 132–4). In line with such observations on the difficulties of removing violence completely from disobedient civil acts, *Oğuz* also highlights the following:

> In essence, there is violence within life itself. I understand non-violence as purification from violence. For me, there is no absolute non-violence. I am talking to you today; maybe there is violence even in my speech, and I will notice this later. That is why it is necessary to question everything: 'Am I currently resorting to violence?', 'how can I deal with the violence that I encounter?' or 'how can I solve it [this problem] without resorting to violence?'

Violence is not limited to physical acts directed at human bodies; violence is beyond such a narrow understanding. First of all, higher moral convictions might justify an act of disobedience that violates *prima facie* rights. For instance, in the case of activists destroying draft files to express the view that war is immoral, the 'government's right not to have its records damaged has been superseded' (Morreall 1991: 139). *Bülent* also differentiates between violence against human beings, which he condemns at all costs, and violence against material objects. He supports 'using violence to destroy war machines'. His willingness to resort to violence to eliminate the 'effectiveness' of war machines yet not to harm human beings reveals that even though disobedience through a non-violent act must be preferred to disobedience through a violent act, there might be occasions that necessarily involve violence to eliminate things considered by conscientious objectors as wrong (Raz 1979: 267). These occasions and their limits should be determined carefully. Conversely, restricting the definition and the scope of civil disobedience and excluding various acts of disobedience limit the opportunity to monitor such acts (Walzer 1970: 25).

Objectors Expose Themselves to 'Civil Death' . . . But Is Acceptance of Punishment Necessary?

According to Rawls (1999: 322), one of the signs of sincerity is the willingness to 'pay a certain price to convince others that our actions have, in our carefully considered view, a sufficient moral basis in the political convictions of the community'. Conscientious objectors in Turkey do indeed 'pay a certain price', exposing themselves to 'civil death'. They are attentive to Turkey's political, cultural and legal structure, which makes any criticism aimed at the military and national duty challenging. They are also aware that, with their declaration, they enter murky territory where they face the risk of prosecution or social exclusion. For instance, when talking about the risk of prosecution under Article 318 and the consequences of conscientious objection, *Ebrari* refers to the years between 2004 and 2008:

> When I declared my objection in 2004, I was tried and put in a military prison. After I was released, a warrant was issued against me. I would be detained and taken to the military. I was taken into custody 4 times in total; I spent 17 months in a military prison. This process continued until 2008. For 4 years, I was a deserter or else in a military prison from time to time.

It is noteworthy that, after 2008, Turkey changed its policy, as a result of international pressure, and conscientious objectors cannot now be taken into the military by force. An objector who undergoes a routine and random identity check by the police would receive an administrative fine. *Ercan*, smiling, mentions that he has received around 30–40 administrative fines so far. On the other hand, *Burak* already knows that they are not in a position to pay these fines, so would not mind receiving more. He says: 'None of us has a financial gain; what could they take from us?'

Even though the objectors are not taken into the military by force, the 'civil death' of objectors reveals itself differently. Objectors avoid going into any governmental offices, yet they still encounter the police either at a random identity check or when they stay in hotels. Almost all interviewees mentioned this point. For example, *Bülent* states that:

> Two years ago, around 5 am, the police came to the hotel where I was staying. They asked me to sign a document stating that I should enlist in the army within 15 days. I said I am a conscientious objector and I do not want to sign. I explained to them what conscientious objection is, but I signed it after debating with them for half an hour. I wrote in the document that I was a conscientious objector, that I was against war for humanitarian, political and philosophical reasons, and would not do military service.

Even though, in the case of conscientious objection, the 'price' that dissenters pay is being repeatedly subjected to 'civil death' in their daily life, it does indeed mean 'voluntary acceptance of (a single) punishment'.

This acceptance indicates that dissenters usually recognise the punishment that follows because they respect the law when they commit the act of disobedience. By submitting themselves to this punishment, dissenters not only express their sincerity but also attract public attention (Cohen 1966: 6). *Oğuz*, for instance, highlights how conscientious objectors are ready to accept the consequences of their refusal:

> Objectors are willing to face the consequences of their actions. For example, Mehmet Bal, a conscientious objector, came to trial with his luggage to indicate that he is ready to go to prison and had no intention of running away. Another striking example is Murat Ulke, who holds dual citizenship (Turkish–German) and stayed in Turkey; he did not run away to Germany. The objectors' act involves all the elements of civil disobedience.

Regarding *Oğuz's* statement, it should be noted that not all objectors respond in the same way. Conscientious objectors can seek refugee status abroad but continue their struggle through other means, such as using social or traditional media, attending workshops or engaging with policymakers at the international level. In these circumstances, the objectors' unwillingness to face the legal consequences of their refusal does not necessarily mean that they aim at destroying the legal system; nor does it mean that it changes the nature of their disobedient acts. Indeed, 'the punishment for an offence may be the very thing that the disobedient opposes' (Brownlee 2016: 967). For instance, conscientious objectors in Turkey consider Article 318 of the Turkish Criminal Code as both the main source and the result of the militarisation of society. Their lack of interest in accepting punishment under Article 318 would not mean that they 'lack fidelity to law'.

It comes as no surprise that Rawls's 'voluntary acceptance of punishment', just like any other elements of civil disobedience, invited considerable criticism. As demonstrated by Maeve Cooke and Danielle Petherbridge (2016: 955), Arendt argues that the purpose of civil disobedience is to allow individuals to participate in political debates. Highlighting the political nature of civil disobedience, she contends that those who are disobedient should voluntarily submit themselves to punishment. For her, disobedient acts should be perceived in a political, rather than a legal, context. Similarly, voluntary acceptance of the legal consequences of disobedience does not apply to all acts of civil disobedience. In some cases, the effectiveness of dissent might require an act which is committed in secrecy. For example, if dissenters who help fugitive slaves to escape accept punishment and act openly, they might jeopardise any future attempts to help others (Greenawalt 1991: 186). It is also argued that although Rawls sees the voluntary acceptance of punishment as a sign of sincerity and, in this sense, dissenters are required to make it clear that they are not 'mere criminals', acceptance of punishment is not the only sign of sincerity. For instance, moral law-breakers might seek asylum after committing an act of civil disobedience, yet they actively protest abroad to demonstrate that the law requires reform. They can use the media and other tools to raise public awareness of the 'faults' inherent in the system. In this case, it is not clear why their unwillingness to accept the punishment stipulated by a law that dissenters found repressive would damage their sincerity (Smart and Bedau 1991: 207).

Whether to treat a moral law-breaker differently from other law-breakers is also a matter of dispute. Some argue that since it is unjust to distinguish between a moral law-breaker and a mere law-breaker when the former breaks the law, dissenters must be punished like all law-breakers, whatever their motivations (Cohen 1966: 6–7). In particular, according to those who argue that acceptance of punishment is a vital element in justifying the act of disobedience, 'it is unjust to discriminate either in favour of civil disobedience or against him[her] simply because his[her] act was done knowingly and deliberately' (Cohen 1966: 7). Submission to punishment can be considered a sign of honesty, making it easy to persuade the public. It might also eliminate the possible consequences of the act of refusal, such as the 'frustration, resentment, and insecurity people feel when their interests are jeopardized' (Greenawalt 1991: 187). However, as addressed by Ronald Dworkin (1977: 206), this understanding, which stems from a belief that the disobedient act is 'morally justified, but [. . .] cannot be legally justified', confers on civil disobedience a similar status to lawlessness. The argument in favour of imposing the same punishment and treatment on moral law-breakers is weak in the sense that although it is impossible to tolerate all disobedience, it cannot be asserted that society 'will collapse if it tolerates some'.

Objectors Turn their Personal Story into a Political Story
According to Rawls (1999: 321), 'civil disobedience is a public act. Not only is it addressed to public principles, but it is also done in public. It is engaged in openly with fair notice; it is not covert or secretive.' In some situations, an act of civil disobedience must be committed in public to achieve its aim. This is when the act is aimed at asking the government to change its policies or laws. Therefore, making the government aware of the act might require notifying the government in advance. When the act itself pertains to public matters, such as calling for a change

in policies, publicity is an essential element of this act (Bedau 1961: 655–6). However, one needs to take into consideration the fact that publicity does not necessarily require the identity of the dissenter to be revealed. The publicity of the act and its motivations are sufficient to fulfil the aim (Raz 1979: 265). Furthermore, it should be noted that the requirement for fair notice does not apply to all forms of disobedience. There are some circumstances in which fair notice might have adverse impacts on the act; in this case, publicity of motivations after the committed act will suffice (Smart and Bedau 1991: 206–7).

Parallel to Rawls's definition of civil disobedience as a public act, conscientious objectors in Turkey turn their personal story into a public one. They state their objection via public declarations. *Bülent*'s story is a clear example of objectors' willingness to discuss their motivations with the public and show solidarity with other conscientious objectors. *Bülent* explains the motivations behind his objection as follows:

> Within my politically motivated and anarchist social circle, I was not planning to serve in the army anyway. However, I declared my objection to show solidarity with Mehmet Tarhan, who was imprisoned because of his refusal. I felt that objecting at the personal level is insufficient; therefore, I needed to be politically active.

Bülent's refusal is a reaction to the imprisonment of objectors, and is not just about seeking personal exemption from military duty. Instead of declaring their objection publicly, objectors can basically hide and escape from service without exposing themselves to the risk of prosecution. Their willingness to put themselves at risk clearly indicates that objection is not simply about asking for personal exemption from military duty but about demanding social change. *Bülent*'s motivation for transforming his personal story into a political struggle encourages us to ask the question of whether it is 'possible to establish a political relationship between conscientious objection and civil disobedience' (Toker Kılınç 2009: 69). Joseph Raz (1979: 263) defines civil disobedience as 'a politically motivated breach of law designed either to contribute directly to a change of a law or of a public policy or to express one's protest against, and dissociation from, a law or a public policy'. He further defines conscientious objection as a 'breach of law for the reason that the agent is morally prohibited to obey it, either because of its general character [. . .] or because it extends to certain cases which should not be covered by it' (Raz 1979: 263) Therefore, according to Raz (1979: 264), civil disobedience, as a political act, is directed at achieving a political result, and as a private act, conscientious objection has no such aim since objectors only 'wish to avoid committing moral wrong by obeying a morally bad law'. In the same vein, Rawls (1999: 323) distinguishes between civil disobedience and conscientious refusal, and perceives civil disobedience in a narrow sense. He defines conscientious refusal as 'noncompliance with a more or less direct legal injunction or administrative order'. In this narrow sense, unlike civil disobedience, conscientious refusal is not necessarily grounded in the majority's understanding of justice. Refusal might be based on motivations that are other than political, such as religious or moral (Rawls 1999: 324).

Contrary to this narrow understanding of civil disobedience, all the interviewees pointed out that although their objection has personal significance, it is, in a broader sense, part of a movement requesting social change. Their narratives illustrate that conscientious objection is a result of inner feelings and has personal facets. Yet conscientious objection has wider implications locating it within the political context. Similarly, *Mehmet* answers the question of what makes the objectors' act, not an individual demand, but rather an act that attempts to bring about a change in society. He states that:

My individual objection is directed at questioning and rejecting the normalisation process, which labels us as women, men, Muslim and Christian. All these labels push you to follow a life that is shaped by others. When it comes to questioning these stereotypes, we – all objectors – stand alone. That is why I first consider my attempt as individualistic. Yet, our individual stands are becoming part of a movement.

Conscientious beliefs are defined as a reflection of 'an individual's inward conviction of what is morally right or morally wrong, and it is a conviction that is genuinely reached and held after some process of thinking about the subject' (Major 1992: 350). Therefore, any objection based on conscientious grounds is perceived as a pretext to gain a personal benefit, such as 'preserving one's selfhood, moral integrity and subjective value' (Toker Kılınç 2009: 61). Therefore, a subjective and personal meaning is attached to conscience in which it is assumed that objectors decide not to fulfil the obligation of the law only when it has detrimental effects on their personal and moral integrity (Toker Kılınç 2009: 62).

Indeed, the aim of preserving moral integrity stood out in a conversation with *Serdar*. He explained, in detail, his transformation from a religious and nationalist person to someone who questions all these well-established discourses of such an environment. For him, it was a difficult job to decide whether to keep on serving in the army or declare an objection. 'I was at a crossroad; I had my family on one side and being lonely on the other side. Then I told myself: I must do it for myself, how would I look at my grandkids' face, otherwise.' Compared to other interviewees, *Serdar*'s initial motivation was more personal, yet this did not prevent him from being part of the movement. Indeed, he was one of the founders of the Association of Conscientious Objection.

Personal motivations behind conscientious objection do not change the fact that most dissenters form their opinions after recognising the best way for them to live. Dissenters' desire to find a political and social environment in which they can live in accordance with their personal motivations cannot be ignored. That is to say, although conscience is a result of an individual's inner convictions, that does not mean it cannot gain a meaningful place within the public space. Walzer (1970: 131) perceives conscience in a broader sense 'as a form of moral knowledge that we share not with God, but with other men [sic] – our fellow citizens, for example, or our comrades or brethren in some movement, party, or sect'. Therefore, he considers the 'description of conscience as "merely personal" inadequate' (Walzer 1970: 130). He states that:

> Men [sic] who continually worry that their objection is a piece of self-indulgence, or who ask over and over and over again whether they are 'really helping the Movement,' or 'working effectively to stop the war,' [. . .] are obviously not acting on the basis of a 'merely personal' code. (Walzer 1970: 130)

Walzer's observations figure prominently in the conscientious objectors' struggle in Turkey. For instance, *Burak* considers his objection an act of civil disobedience in the sense that the act itself is directed at bringing about change. He highlights how dissenters cooperate with other associations such as those who work on animal rights violations, war and militarism. The aim is to promote the idea of refusing compulsory military service and also raise awareness of animal rights because they believe that war destroys nature and animals. *Burak*'s attempt at forging a link between militarism and animal rights in making sense of his conscientious objection indicates that his aim is not simply to obtain an individual exemption from military duty.

Gökhan also believes that 'if the individual is not free, society is not free, and vice versa. Although our objection has personal motivations, it needs to be directed at transforming society. I cannot make any distinction between them.' *Gökhan*'s reference to the transformation of society illustrates how conscientious objectors might base their refusal on moral principles which might apply to a great number of individuals. In this sense, objectors not only disobey the law to avoid committing an act that goes against their moral convictions but also challenge the system (Sagi and Shapira 2002: 184). Accordingly, when objectors challenge the state, they do not 'make their claims on the basis of "merely personal" codes, but on the basis of shared principles and mutual engagements' (Walzer 1970: 131). Therefore, in cases where conscientious objectors consider their objection as part of a movement and locate their argument within a discussion of war, militarism, patriarchy and so on, categorising their objection as a 'merely' private act would have detrimental impacts on the legitimacy of their wider demands that go beyond gaining a personal exemption from military service. Such a categorisation would also limit the scope of the right to conscientious objection.

Finally, as pointed out by Kimberley Brownlee (2012: 12), both terms are associated with meaningful values. Like civil disobedience, conscientious objection raises noteworthy demands of 'personal convictions', which are protected by the law in just societies. Both acts involve a serious and sincere refusal of what people consider wrong. In certain situations, conscientious objection might be considered an act of civil disobedience. To illustrate, conscientious objection might be the product of moral convictions, focusing on the wrongness of engaging in any war-making process or being involved in any part of such law, regardless of whether it recognises a right to conscientious objection. Objectors may also refuse to apply for conscientious objector status because they believe that making such an appeal means accepting the state's authority to enact laws on a war-making process. Therefore, they refuse to cooperate with these laws in any way or even ask for an exemption.[2] In this case, a deliberate refusal of regulations, particularly those pertaining to military conscription, is a form of civil disobedience (Cohen 1968: 271–2).

Objectors' Public Refusal is Legitimate
According to Rawls (1999: 320–1), a

> civilly disobedient act is indeed thought to be contrary to law, at least in the sense that those engaged in it are not simply presenting a test case for a constitutional decision; they are prepared to oppose the statute even if it should be upheld.

During the interviews, conscientious objectors classified their objection as civil disobedience by highlighting the legitimacy of their objection.

Burak was very clear about the distinction between an illegal and a legitimate act:

> You cannot gain legitimacy just by gaining legal acceptance. In a similar vein, not all illegal acts can be regarded as illegitimate. Therefore, the lack of legal recognition has no impacts on the legitimacy of our actions. It is an international right. Furthermore, we are in cooperation with both international and national organisations.

In parallel with *Burak*'s point, *Ercan* highlights the legitimacy of their actions. He illustrates his point by reference to solidarity among objectors in the case of prosecutions. He says this:

> Let's assume fifty citizens are taken into custody at the same time, and just one of them is a conscientious objector; the headline of the news would be that 'forty-nine individuals and a conscientious objector are taken into custody'. We have such visibility as a result of cooperating with international organisations, namely War Resisters' International (WRI) and Akdeniz Meeting in Cyprus. In the case of prosecutions of objectors, these institutions are informed of the situation quickly. That is what makes our act, if not legal, legitimate.

Davut captures the similarities between civil disobedience and conscientious objection by referring to the legitimacy of their objection:

> Individuals who develop the attitude of objection are aware that they are getting involved in an illegal act and are, therefore, ready to face the consequences of their actions. They base their argument on the legitimacy of their actions. Furthermore, they publicly and openly refuse to serve. In this sense, their acts can be considered as an act of civil disobedience.

It is also worth analysing whether acts of dissidence can be considered acts of civil disobedience when the legality of the norms is questioned before the high court. For instance, with regard to unconstitutionality claims, there is a debate over whether an act is illegal if the court rules that the law is not compatible with the Constitution (Rawls 1999: 321). For instance, William Taylor, General Counsel for the United States Commission on Civil Rights, suggests that

> if a violation [of law] is committed under a claim of legal right with the intention of seeking redress in the courts, it can hardly be termed civil disobedience.

> In fact, under our judicial system, it is frequently necessary to violate the law to vindicate one's legal rights. If the person challenging a law as unconstitutional cannot show that [s]he has violated it, the courts may say that the case is a hypothetical one which is not ripe for decision. (MacGuigan 1971: 254–5)

Carl Cohen (1966: 8) similarly argues that 'when the challenge to the constitutionality (or constitutional applicability) of a law is unsuccessful, there is disobedience but not legal justification. Where such a challenge is successful, there is legal justification, but no disobedience.' This understanding underestimates the circumstances and the motivations of dissenters during the act of civil disobedience (MacGuigan 1971: 225). In some cases, dissenters might object to the law because it contradicts their fundamental and constitutional rights. Even though dissenters are challenging the government, their acts are not directed at determining the legitimacy of the policy or the law. Determining whether the law is legal remains as yet in the hands of the authorities. Therefore, regardless of whether the dissenters' acts are within the scope of constitutional rights, these acts still need to be considered as acts of civil disobedience (Bedau 1961: 655).

Conclusion

> The act is non-violent. The most important aspect of the civil disobedience act is that it reveals the will of the individual. For instance, the standing man's resistance in the Gezi protests [where a man stood motionless and silent for six hours during protests in Turkey against police brutality] is a clear example of civil disobedience. Although it was an act committed by just a single person, it had more impact than any other acts involving a great deal of people. The stand of the conscientious objectors is the same. What refusal reveals is the will of the individual. In this sense, it is precious. It has the aim of delivering a social message. (interview with *Oğuz*)

This book embraces a broad definition of conscientious objection as a tool used to question society's militarist structures; therefore, this chapter has focused on the similarities between civil disobedience and conscientious objection to clarify whether conscientious objection is an act of civil disobedience. It has forged a link between civil disobedience and conscientious objection by arguing that conscientious objection is not limited to refusing a duty and demanding a personal exemption from military service. When conscientious objectors refuse the militarisation of society, they aim at bringing about change. In brief, a conscientiously motivated act is seen as a personal act. However, most of the conscientious declarations are read in public in order to engage in open debates and encourage public participation. Objectors' public declarations open a discussion about militarism; thus, conscientious objection to military service takes the form of a collective act rather than an individual one. When the objection rests on ideas such as criticising the state, challenging its militarist implementations and questioning the social structure, conscientious objection should also be considered a political act, not only a moral or personal one (Toker Kılınç 2009: 69–70).

Notes

1. Rawls uses the term 'conscientious refusal' (instead of 'conscientious objection'), defined as 'noncompliance with a more or less direct legal injunction or administrative order'. He further indicates that 'unwillingness of a pacifist to serve in the armed forces, or of a soldier to obey an order that he thinks is manifestly contrary to the moral law as it applies to war, the refusal of the Jehovah's Witnesses to salute the flag constitutes a conscientious refusal' (see Rawls 1999: 323–4). Hence, the term 'conscientious refusal' is used in a way that includes conscientious objection to military service as well. In this study, 'conscientious refusal' and 'conscientious objection' will be employed interchangeably.

2. For instance, Mehmet Tarhan, an LGBTQI activist and objector in Turkey, rejected exemption from military service based on regulations on LGBTQIs and military service. In his conscientious objection declaration, he stated that 'the report that classifies me as "unfit" (or "rotten") because I am gay and affords me the "right" to exemption from military service is nothing more than a sign of the rottenness of the state itself' (see 'The Case of Conscientious Objector Mehmet Tarhan'. Available at: <http://www.wri-irg.org/node/1585> (last accessed 21 October 2015). When objectors who base their refusal on their sexual identity will not apply for exemption in a society that prohibits LGBTQIs from military service, on the understanding that homosexuality is a disease, their action takes the form of a collective act.

CHAPTER 6

Curious Women Conscientious Objectors to Military Service in the Male Conscription System in Turkey

Introduction

Beware the adjective 'trivial.' Beware 'normal'.

(Enloe 2016: 25)

Militarism is everywhere. It is in our daily life, in our childhood memories and toys, and in the language we speak. Questions thus arise as to how militarism is normalised through establishing and maintaining gender roles. How is such normalisation being challenged? To forge the link between gender and militarism, this chapter studies women's conscientious objection to military service in Turkey. It utilises Cynthia Enloe's (2004: 220) feminist curiosity, 'a curiosity that provokes serious questioning about the workings of masculinized and feminized meanings'. Developing a feminist curiosity, while providing insights into the conscientious objection movement in Turkey, is crucial to making sense of women's conscientious objection in the male conscription system, understanding conscientious objection from a wider perspective and unveiling the tools used to integrate militarism into society.

Since women are not subject to conscription in Turkey, they are likely to be seen as irrelevant to the matter. They are ironically asked a common question: you are not conscripted, so why do you refuse? This cynical approach to women's objection not only creates a male-dominated environment around antimilitarist views but also ignores the multiple purposes behind the act of refusal. The aim of this chapter is, therefore, to discuss how the link between gender and militarism is understood in the context of Turkey, a country that still has a system of male conscription. It illustrates how conscription constitutes only one dimension of militarism and how militarism also affects women's lives, even though they are not subject to compulsory military service. In so doing, the chapter broadens the discussion on the right to conscientious objection by studying those who have previously been assumed to be 'irrelevant'.

The analysis proceeds as follows: the first section presents the theoretical framework, first by engaging with the broad discussion on the normalisation of militarism through gender norms in general, then by exploring the link between gender and militarism in the context of Turkey. The second section provides empirical evidence coupled with a gender analysis to show how militarism is understood and challenged in Turkey. With a particular focus on the necessity to raise feminist questions, the chapter concludes by arguing that a gendered reading of militarism makes its invisible aspects visible and challenges what is considered normal and unquestionable.

Gender and Militarism

Gender's Role in the Normalisation of Militarism

> Gender roles adapt individuals for war roles, and war roles provide the context within which individuals are socialized into gender roles. (Sjoberg and Via 2010: 6)

The military as an institution embraces different values and embodies different priorities compared to civil institutions. For instance, to counter any criticism, the military gives a dominantly honourable meaning to death by constructing myths and discourses (Kovitz 2003). In their analysis of militarism in the British context, Rachel Woodward and Trish Winter (2007: 100) state that 'discourses are fundamental because they give meaning to a material reality, they make things "real". Discursive practices bring the Army into being; they are how we imagine the Army into existence.' That is to say, although the military is visible and such visibility is embodied in the presence of soldiers, weapons and troops, the meaning attributed to them and the rationale for their existence are shaped by discursive practices, and it is only via these that the military gains society's support (Woodward and Winter 2007). Similarly, Victoria Basham (2015) observes that convincing young people to use force and legitimising wars depend on how these practices are normalised in everyday life. Such normalisation is achieved primarily through emotions that are directed at constructing a national consciousness, so as to ensure young people's voluntary participation in the operation of military and national defence.

Generally speaking, the dichotomy of manliness versus womanliness is one of the causes contributing to the normalisation of militarism. While the former conceptualises men as naturally violent, the latter conceptualises women as naturally peaceful (Carden-Coyne 2012; Yuval-Davis 1997). It is vital to take into consideration the fact that, during conflicts, the protection of national security is prioritised over human rights, especially when it comes to gender equality. For this reason, women's endeavour for peace is also a struggle for gender equality and the demilitarisation of society. However, this does not necessarily mean that women's demand for peace is the product of their 'peaceful nature'. Assuming that the existence of a connection between all women and pacifism only contributes to bolstering stereotypes, such as 'women are more caring than men' (Golan 1997: 584). Women become involved in the peace movement for all sorts of motivations and reasons rather than just that of being peaceful mothers, a role assigned to them by society (Yuval-Davis 1997). Therefore, this chapter forges a link between militarism and gender, not because women are peaceful, but because militarism maintains its power through gendered understandings and myths.

The portrayal of women as 'the protected' and men as 'the protectors' also enhances militarism. This dichotomy, on the one hand, qualifies 'the protector' to speak for others and to gain a place in the public sphere; on the other hand, it confines 'the protected' to the domestic sphere, making them perceive themselves as weak and, consequently, accept that they are silenced (Enloe 2016). Such a dichotomy also gives women certain roles to play as the mothers, wives and girlfriends of soldiers. For example, one of the prominent tools used to maintain manpower and keep up the citizens' spirit to fight for the nation is the dichotomy of unpatriotic versus patriotic motherhood. Glorification of patriotic motherhood involves accepting the sacrifice of sons without questioning it (Zeiger 1996). The patriotic mother is expected to ease her pain with the honour of sacrificing her son's life for the sake of the nation. Therefore, there is a close connection between the soldier and the patriotic mother, in a sense that they share common characteristics, such as being subjected to orders and hierarchy without questioning and having the will to sacrifice their life (Zeiger 1996). This connection indicates that the construction of women as the weaker sex – 'the protected' – by overemphasising their biological differences is followed by the construction of mother–son ties. As a result, soldiers view military service as a way to protect their mothers from any kind of threat.

Women's roles and the stereotypes around these roles in the normalisation process are hard to escape. As Nira Yuval-Davis (1997: 93) explains,

'militaries and warfare [militarism] have never been just a "male zone".
Women have always fulfilled certain, often vital, roles within them.' Militarism, as an on-going process, needs women's cooperation as mothers,
wives or workers to normalise the militarisation process and to make
both men and women believe that they have certain responsibilities and
roles (Cockburn 2013). In Britain, for example, women contributed to
the war effort during World War I. They took over men's jobs so that
they could join the army instead, acted as nurses and actively encouraged men to participate in the on-going war (Bibbings 2003). In fact,
a number of women delivered a white feather to civilian men as a sign
of cowardice (Enloe 2009). However, it is worth noting that although
women's contribution to the war effort was not an official policy of the
British government (in fact, women acted independently, just like other
women who opposed the war), the idea of delivering a white feather was
a product of war propaganda.

War propaganda is defined as 'the control of opinion by significant
symbols or, to speak more concretely and less accurately, by stories,
rumours, reports, pictures and other forms of social communication'
(quoted in Lutz 1933: 497). Controlling public opinion and gaining
public support are considered important parts of the war effort (Lutz
1933). For instance, during World War I, posters occupied an important
role in increasing citizens' participation in the war effort. Through lyri-
cal expressions of war on low-priced and easily distributed posters, war
administrators contrived to gain public support. They reached wider segments of society and influenced their daily life and outlook on war. These
posters were part of the routine of daily life and were constant reminders
of an individual's duty to participate in the war (Shover 1975). The war
posters were not independent of the cultural characteristics of a given
society; they had culturally familiar connotations that affected society's
perception of gender roles and war. These posters used simple language
and included familiar, positive and non-threatening images. In other
words, the devastating effects of war were replaced by images of suppos-
edly 'naïve' and 'pure' women (Shover 1975).

On such posters, women were appointed as guardians of the process
of enlisting manpower, as clearly indicated by the 'Women of Britain
say – "GO!"' poster. Women voluntarily convinced men to enlist and
also ridiculed those who refused to do so using language that under-
mined their masculinity (Shover 1975; Kumar 2004). Examples of such
language, which prevailed on war posters, include: 'Will you go or must
I?', 'I WANT YOU – for THE NAVY', 'IF YOU WANT TO FIGHT! – JOIN
THE MARINES', 'GEE!! I WISH I WERE A MAN – I'D JOIN THE NAVY'

(Shover 1975: 482). The messages embedded in the posters indicated that women needed to give the spirit of their husbands, sons and boyfriends the moral uplift to join the army: they 'needed to free the men' (Yesil 2004: 109). Such posters, which reflect the assumed roles that women play as mothers, wives and supporters of soldiers, demonstrate that women are not entirely excluded from the military. Yet, their presence, contribution and expected roles are enmeshed in gender norms (Kumar 2004).

Curious Women Conscientious Objectors in Turkey

In the 1990s, Tayfun Gönül and Vedat Zencir introduced the idea of conscientious objection in Turkey by declaring their conscientious objection to compulsory military service, motivated by their conscientious and political beliefs. They did so in a politically sensitive atmosphere, since the effects of the 1980 military coup were still being felt. Despite the difficulties in refusing military service in politically sensitive times, conscientious objection in Turkey gradually gained public attention (Çınar and Üsterci 2009b). In 1992, the War Resisters' Association was founded in Izmir, Turkey, with the aim of challenging militarism and attracting the public's attention. According to its official charter, one of the goals of the Association was 'being against militarism'. Indeed, the Association was asked to remove this statement from the charter, as the authorities believed that militarism was not an issue in Turkey. This demand was refused on the grounds that removing the statement would go against the fundamental purpose of the Association. The Association was, consequently, dissolved but was later refounded under the name of the Association of Izmir War Resisters, with more members this time. It encouraged collective conscientious objection declarations and organised international meetings in solidarity with conscientious objectors. In 1994, another branch of the War Resisters' Association was established in Istanbul (Üsterci and Yorulmaz 2009c). Over time, more objectors declared their conscientious objection, and among them the case of Osman Murat Ülke is considered one of the turning points of conscientious objection in Turkey. The European Court of Human Rights declared that repeated prosecution of objectors amounts to 'civil death'.[1] With this case, the matter was brought to public scrutiny (Çınar and Üsterci 2009b). Since then, the number of conscientious objectors has gradually been increasing. Here, the question that needs to be asked is 'where are the women' within this movement (Enloe 2009)?

Even though the feminist movement has gained momentum since the 1980s and women have started to become involved in conscientious objection movements, up until 2004 their involvement was considered as merely 'supporting' the conscientious objectors. Finally, women started to declare their objection in 2004, thus becoming 'active members' of the movement rather than being 'supportive wives/mothers/sisters' (Altınay 2009). 'Their conscientious objection created a climate of confusion and curiosity in public, particularly about the role that gender plays in the militarization process' (Caltekin 2018: 1). The question that arises is if women are not subject to conscription, why are they objecting? To answer this, women conscientious objectors focused on the following reasons behind their refusal: first, militarism affects not only men but women too; and second, it is vital to challenge what has been considered to be 'normal'.

We (Women) Object Because . . .

We are Affected and Militarism Needs Women Too

> To refuse the source of the ongoing oppression, we do not need to be subjected to conscription. We argue that conscientious objection is a women's right as women are the most affected by militarism. Even though the military does not explicitly ask us to serve in the army, it already includes us in the system by seeing us as a nest that will give birth to soldiers and also by expecting us to say 'long live the homeland (*vatan sağolsun*)' when the soldier gets killed. While the system expects us to beat a drum at the funeral, to say 'today is my son's wedding day', we do not need to be included in the army because we already are. That is the reason why women declare their objection.

Atlas's words are based on her book, entitled *Kişer Pari Mama:2 Kadınlar Savaşı Reddediyor* (*Kişer Mami Papa: Women are Rejecting War*), in which she conducted interviews with twenty-one women conscientious objectors (Arslan 2015). *Atlas*, as a journalist, decided to study women objectors to understand their stories and make their voice heard. Her interaction with these women made her observe the militarisation process and develop different strategies to question it. She says that

> upon completion of the book, I was transformed into someone else. I was not only a journalist, but one who approaches antimilitarism from a very different perspective. As a result of such transformation, I declared my objection on International Conscientious Objection Day (15 May 2015).

In addition to summarising the common denominators among women objectors and capturing the integration of militarism in women's daily life, *Atlas*'s narrative illustrates how the invisible roots of militarism affect women and produce societal expectations. Her reference to the perceptions of women as patriot citizens shows us how women's lives can be shaped by militarist expectations. It also explains why women's refusal is considered as part of the conscientious objection movement, even though they are not subject to compulsory military service. Yet, *Atlas*'s claim that 'women are the most affected by militarism' merits clarification. War not only glorifies manhood or produces heroes but also puts men's life at risk and subjects them to violence, rape or other kinds of ill-treatment (Charlesworth 2008). Therefore, the main point behind stressing the impacts of war and militarism on women's life is not to claim that women suffer more than men, but that war is not only about men.

This point is illustrated by *Didem*. She states that 'we, women, are here too and affected by war'. *Didem* considers her objection as an obligation because there were not many women conscientious objectors in 2013–14. She goes on to say that 'I was so impressed when I heard that women use menstrual blood as a means of resistance. This serves the purpose of raising women's visibility [not only in public but in war/peace discussions].' In her view, women objectors are 'the menstrual blood left in the middle of a war zone'. *Didem*'s awareness of symbolic ways of resisting made her declare her objection on International Women's Day. However, this is not peculiar to *Didem*; women strategically decide to declare their objection on either International Women's Day or International Conscientious Objection Day to raise awareness of the link between gender and militarism and also to make women's experiences of militarism visible and relevant.

Atlas's and *Didem*'s reference to the ways in which militarism shapes the lives of women, either directly or indirectly, is indicative of how women's conscientious objection is directed not only at compulsory military service, but also at militarisation of their daily lives. In their narratives, women conscientious objectors also illustrate how militarism has an agenda that has an impact on men's lives and shapes women's attitude to normalise the militarisation process. This is symptomatic of the idea that militarism needs women too. Women conscientious objectors also constantly refer to women's given roles in the militarisation process: being patriotic mothers and loyal and grateful wives, 'accepting' a vulnerable position, as opposed to their counterparts who enjoy protector status in the family.

Zeynep's motivations behind her objection show a similarity to *Didem's*. In her view, 'in patriarchal societies, women are expected to give birth to a boy, and once they have done so, they are exalted [. . .] war is made possible by discourses on women and children'. In this sense, she, like *Didem*, considers her objection as 'a slap in the face of militarism – a voice bursting out that I am a woman and not obligated to give birth – and a refusal to cooperate with the system'. *Zeynep's* position, which links reasons of war with gender, mirrors Cynthia Cockburn's (2010) argument, which considers gender as a cause of war.

During the interview, *Zeynep* also makes a critical comment: 'To understand any phenomenon, it is so common to consider its most obvious, tangible and direct elements. Yet, we, women, burst out the opposite and say: We are here too.' *Zeynep's* motivations that aim to consider the hidden or abstract elements of militarism reveal that women activists, while challenging war and militarism, 'bring gender relations into the picture not as an alternative but as an intrinsic, interwoven, inescapable part of the very same story' (Cockburn 2010: 140).

We Want to Refuse the So-called 'Normal' and Speak Out About What Is Hidden

Women conscientious objectors refuse militarism by questioning any notion that relates gender roles with biology to normalise them. This point recurred in the narratives of almost all the women objectors. For example, *Meltem Nur* confronts the normalisation of unequal distribution of household chores by explicitly linking it with military service. She does not remember the year in which she objected, saying that 'years and dates are not important. Yet, I specifically chose International Conscientious Objection Day as women's objection is a tool used to raise awareness and make people question why a woman would declare an objection while she is not conscripted.' The starting point of her critique is grounded in her curiosity to question the gendered roles in her family and the relationship between such roles and militarism. She believes that 'household chores are equivalent to men's military duty, in a sense that both of them have become normal and unquestionable'. During the interview, she recalls a memory of her mother, the figure of a woman in their house who accepted her role as a mother and as a wife: 'I recall my mother working in the kitchen and when she needed any help, she just used to call me but not her two sons, who also used to sit in the living room.' Such moments, in which *Meltem Nur* became aware of the unequal distribution of housework in her family, led her to develop a feminist curiosity and to question gender norms.

Didem's feminist curiosity is the product of her first encounter with militarism. During the interview, she evokes a memory in which she was planning to apply for the military high-school exams. She smiles and says, 'such a contradiction, isn't it?' Then, she narrates her story: 'I collected the army's leaflet with excitement; however, shortly after I noticed that male students only were allowed to apply, I started questioning *every-thing.*' *Didem* considers this moment as a turning point in her life that led to the gradual development of a feminist curiosity which shifted her position from dreaming of being a soldier to declaring her objection instead.

Women objectors deploy their feminist curiosity and ask: why would women be considered peaceful? Does biology determine whether you are peaceful? They believe that the perception of women as naturally peaceful plays an essential role in normalising the militarisation process. *Özlem Dede*, a student who had declared her objection on 10 July 2016, right before I interviewed her, identifies herself as an anarchist and a feminist, and her family as oppositional. She believes that 'women are *shaped* by the political power (*iktidar, erk*) as peaceful and naïve to fit in male-dominant systems. They are assigned this artificial peaceful nature as a result of the socialisation process. Therefore, it is not biological.' Following this statement, *Özlem* brings up a critical point that has been discussed in war and gender studies:

> Killing in war does not come naturally for either gender, yet the potential for war has been universal in human societies. To help overcome soldiers' reluctance to fight, cultures develop gender roles that equate 'manhood' with toughness under fire. Across cultures and through time, the selection of men as potential combatants (and of women for feminine war support roles) has helped shape the war system. In turn, pervasiveness of war in history has influenced gender profoundly, especially gender norms in child-rearing. (Goldstein 2003: 9)

In general, the main point of *Özlem's* argument figures prominently in Enloe's work, which runs against 'taking things for granted', instead calling attention to and questioning what is seen as natural or trivial (Enloe 2007: 24–5). It can be seen that women conscientious objectors debate the merits of militarism by employing their feminist curiosity, thus challenging gendered stereotypes.

We Want to Challenge the Integration of Militarism into Society

Since women in Turkey are not subject to conscription, their voices are likely to be seen as irrelevant to the issue. This was a recurring theme among the women conscientious objectors. During the interviews, they mainly talked about how people are confused about women's objection. For example, *Zeynep* mentions that her family could not make sense of her objection or that of any other woman conscientious objector: 'When I was detained for showing solidarity with Enver Aydemir, an objector who faced inhuman treatment, their [my family's] first reaction was: "You are not going to be a soldier. Why are you objecting?"' While discussing her objection with her family and with anyone who has difficulties in understanding women's objection, *Zeynep* says:

At the micro level, the common understanding that women need to get married at a certain age and give birth to a son is part of the militarist agenda. The myths that present heaven as a prize for fertile women and exalt mothers while portraying infertile women as incomplete are the invisible facets of militarism.[3] Similarly, portraying the nation as women and MOTHERland (ANAvatan) puts men in a position where they need to protect their mothers from all kinds of threats. At this point, militarism interferes with women's daily lives through honour myths. In short, the effects of militarism on women can be read via these invisible facets of militarism that link the nation with honour and women.

Zeynep, like other female conscientious objectors in Turkey, aims to understand militarism's impacts on society at a broader level by being curious about its sociological and cultural connotations. Another example of the sociological facets of militarism is provided by *Ebru Altıntaş*, who decided to declare her objection after her women friend committed suicide. *Ebru* read her declaration on 10 July 2016, just before I interviewed her. She considers her objection as part of women's struggles in real life, and identifies herself as an anarchist and her family as not politically active. She gives examples about the sociological aspects of military service by referring to a school ceremony in Turkey:

Since I was born, I was raised as a soldier even though I was not given a gun. When I started my education at the age of seven, I stood up like a soldier in the school line and was asked to march and say: 'I am a Turk, may my presence be sacrificed for the existence of the Turkish nation!' I was put in a position in which I can sacrifice my presence for any circumstances or sacrifice my son or husband. Therefore, I grounded my objection on the effects of

militarism on social life. My objection is directed not only at refusing the use
of guns but also at militarism in general.

Ebru's statement exemplifies how, within gendered and militarised societies, individuals encounter the dichotomy of manliness versus womanliness at an early age through children's games and toys, as well as in
advertisements on social and mainstream media (Cockburn 2013). *Ebru*
also shows how women's feminist curiosity comes into play to question
such routinised ceremonies. Without being curious about why students
are compelled to 'sacrifice [their] presence', it would not be possible to
challenge the way militarism indoctrinates the lives of people with masculinised values even before they enlist. That is why one of the school
songs that imposes social norms on children in a subtle way has been
scrutinised by curious feminists. The song runs as follows:

> Little 'Ayşe', Little 'Ayşe',
> Tell me what you are doing,
> I am taking care of my baby,
> I am singing lullabies to it.
> Little 'soldier', little 'soldier',
> Tell me what you are doing,
> I am taking care of my rifle
> I am attaching a bayonet to it. (Altinay 2009: 92)

The song shows that these gendered practices strengthen the connection
between militarism and masculinity and proves that 'a strategy for demil-
itarization and peace must include a strategy of change in masculinities' (Duncanson 2015: 232). For that reason, this chapter approaches
militarism through the eyes of those who want a change in masculinities
and reject the performance of gendered roles. It considers the relationship between men and women rather than adopting an approach which
focuses only on women. As gender relations have a mutual impact on
one another, they therefore require a two-sided investigation (Cockburn
and Žarkov 2002). That is to say, it is essential to 'explore women's full
range of relationship to men' (Enloe 2009: 81). For this reason, having
examined women conscientious objectors' justifications for their objection, the chapter now moves to the question of how men perceive wom-
en's objection to compulsory military service.[4] To answer this question,
male objectors focused on the following points: first, militarism does not
affect soldiers only; and second, a movement composed only of men carries a risk of privileging masculinity.

Women Object Because . . .

Militarisation Does Not Affect Soldiers Only

When becoming a soldier is seen as a sign of becoming a 'real' man and when women are allocated certain roles, such as being patriotic mothers and partners, gendered norms are no longer intrinsic to the army in particular but become integrated into society. This point was illustrated by most of the male conscientious objectors that I interviewed. One of them is *Gökhan*. While talking about the motivations behind his objection, he focuses on his intellectual transformation. In his view, the long process of evaluating socio-cultural/political circumstances and reading about nationalism and gender eventually brought him to the point where he refused compulsory military service. When he talks about his intellectual transformation, he refers to Turkey's constantly changing political agenda: 'We are in Turkey, anything at any time can transform your personality to something else.' *Gökhan* not only describes his objection by referring to his own intellectual transformation but also focuses on the transformation of soldiers' families and explains how mothers are affected by militarism.

> Compulsory military service aims to reshape the individual who has already been shaped by compulsory education. However, the military forms not only the thinking of soldiers but also that of their parents. Soldiers' parents start thinking differently about domestic politics. For instance, parents who used to sympathise with the HDP [Peoples' Democratic Party, the pro-Kurdish opposition party] can transform into parents who hate the Kurds both because of the political atmosphere and because of the fact that their sons are in the army. This is to say, compulsory military service reshapes the thoughts of parents as much as those of the soldiers.

Gökhan's perspective reveals how militarism expands its area of impact by appealing to gender norms and emotions. Similarly, *Bülent,* referring to his father's attempts to convince him to serve in the army, states that

> I have never worn a uniform and never been a soldier. I graduated from university in 1998 and since then I refused to join the army. Yet, in 2005 when they imprisoned Mehmet Tarhan [a conscientious objector], I decided to carry my objection to a political sphere and declared my objection.

It appears that one can consider *Bülent's* objection and that of most of the other objectors as a reaction to the imprisonment of the objectors and as an act of solidarity. He believes that 'conscientious objection cannot be reduced to the refusal to join the army. Gun factories and institutions serving war in indirect ways are part of the war policy.' Focusing on war's cultural and political roots, *Gökhan* similarly notes that 'women's objection is not something exclusively about wartime. War is a culture. War does not happen at once and all of a sudden. Its roots need to grow culturally and politically.'

Gökhan's and *Bülent's* focus is essential as it pays attention to elements that nurture the roots of the problem and it allows us to understand and challenge what lies beneath the surface. Their statements are reminiscent of Joshua Goldstein's definition of war as a *system* which includes both the use of force and preparation for wars mentally and physically (2003), and Laura Sjoberg and Sandra Via's statement that 'war is a tremendously diverse enterprise, operating in many contexts with many purposes, rules, and meanings' (2010: 9). Their stand can also be explained by reference to Cockburn's understanding of war:

> War-fighting between two armies is only the tip of the iceberg, as it were, of an underlying, less immediate, set of institutions and relationships that can be understood as systemic [. . .] Such a systemic view of war readily opens up to gender analysis. Its institutions, let us say the 'military industrial complex', can be seen as loci of several dimensions of power, economic, national – and patriarchal. (Cockburn 2010: 147)

A Movement Composed Only of Men Carries a Risk of Privileging Masculinity

Male conscription systems sustain their 'effectiveness' through the strong relationship between military service and masculinity. In highly militarised societies, men are expected to distance themselves from anything labelled as feminine. The social expectations of men in relation to their identity and manhood compel them to identify themselves with the military and get involved in combat duties (Enloe 1988: 13–14). This is precisely because they fear being labelled as 'feminine' and, as a result, losing respect and occupying a politically weak position (Enloe 2007: 52). Wartime policies need binary oppositions. The dichotomy of women as 'the protected' versus men as 'the protectors' may reveal itself amongst men as the dichotomy of 'heroic' soldier versus 'cowardly' conscientious objector. This binary opposition of 'heroic soldiers' versus 'cowardly conscientious objectors' gives rise to the masculine man versus the feminine man/ unman dichotomy (Bibbings 2003: 337). Portraying war 'as a matter of "duty", "honour", "patriotism", a defence of "freedom" [. . .] then resistance for many men (and women) becomes a matter of cowardice and dishonour' (Nagel 1998: 259).

Conscientious objectors refuse to conform with these masculine features that are exclusively seen as necessary for becoming a 'real' man: to be ready to 'die and kill' and become a 'hero'. They construct their social circle in a manner which allows them to challenge masculinity. During the interviews, almost all of the interviewees answered my questions on 'how did your friends react to your objection and were you labelled as a "coward"?' by emphasising that their friend circle is isolated from militarised and gendered minds, or the fact that they are surrounded by people who share similar views.[5] For instance, *Ercan* indicates, as did others, that 'I have a political identity that creates a field in which my refusal is considered understandable.' *Burak* also stresses that 'my close social circle is open-minded, and you can discuss and talk about most of the issues. Even my apolitical friends know that I am challenging militarism. I have not experienced any accusation of being cowardly or lazy.'

Male conscientious objectors also focus on the necessity of eliminating the risk of privileging masculinity and becoming a male-dominated movement. Their primary motivation behind considering women's refusal as part of the conscientious objection movement is that they believe that a movement composed only of men carries a risk of privileging masculinity (Çınar and Üsterci 2009b). For example, acknowledging such a motivation behind women's conscientious objection, *Halil* raises his concerns over being called a 'hero', even though other objectors and he himself oppose the concept of heroism. In his view:

> Even when they refuse to be part of the war in certain political arenas, men might be labelled as 'heroes' because of their willingness to accept the consequences of their actions. In this respect, for the conscientious movement not to invent heroes, women's involvement in the movement, their criticism of masculinity and their antimilitarist stand are essential and precious.

The statement of *Halil*, the only interviewee who identifies himself as a pacifist, is a clear indication that a gendered understanding exaggerates biological differences in a way which positions (heterosexual) men at the top of the hierarchy among sexes. Both during and after war, men are associated with fighting wars and bringing glory to the nation, hence securing a place in the political arena (Cockburn and Žarkov 2002). Lois Bibbings's (2003: 339) insights on war propaganda during World War I give us a better understanding of how manhood was portrayed in the war context. They also highlight how heroism was used as a tool to gain young people's support for a policy based not only on dying but also on killing – a very often forgotten side of military service. Bibbings argues that military service is portrayed in the media and on recruitment posters as a duty and, more importantly, as an opportunity for men to become 'heroes'. This link between war and heroism (by extension, masculinity) compels activists within the conscientious objection movement to challenge patriarchy and masculinities; otherwise, the movement itself would be transferred into something that reinforces the tenets of militarism (Çınar and Üsterci 2009b). Similarly, *Ercan* asserts that 'solidarity with women, their presence and contributions are important elements that help the movement to preserve its multiplicity and diversity'. Highlighting that he is also a member of a working group focusing on war, trauma and confrontation issues, *Ercan* states that:

> Militarism is actually grounded on the social roles attributed to men and women [. . .] Masculinity is the most problematic aspect of society [. . .] That is the reason why I question masculinity and base my conscientious objection on refusing masculinity. When I give talks, I try to keep the masculinity discussion alive, open it for discussion and create a site of discussion and work on a potential change.

Ercan's effort to link his objection to refusing masculinity is meaningful. It demonstrates that male objectors are attentive to the risks of reproducing masculine norms while refusing military service. Not far from what *Ercan* puts forward, *Davut* also perceives women's involvement in the conscientious objection movement as 'precious in the sense that it helps to overcome the handicap that conscientious objection is the political arena preserved for men'. To clarify the justifications for women's objection to military service, *Davut* makes a critical remark and summarises the main argument among objectors with considerable precision:

> When you evaluate conscientious objection in its restricted sense and consider it only as a legal demand, women's refusal and the fact that women define themselves as the subject of the movement might be found bizarre. However, the foundation of the conscientious objection movement in Turkey is based on political motivations. Politically, it is seen as an arena of opposing militarism and raising voices against war. War is not only a man issue. Furthermore, declarations of objection are not only focused on refusing the duty of military service; they are positioned at refusing the war machine and the militarist system, including the duty of military service. Therefore,

women's involvement in the movement is precious. Conscientious objection
is not an issue of exemption from a duty. It is a demand for the abolishment
of the facts, which urge people to refuse to take part in the military.

Davut's concerns, as a lawyer, regarding the risk of limiting conscientious objection to a legal demand reveals that the fundamental motivations behind the objectors' refusal transcend the individual level, thus
becoming a societal issue. In other words, conscientious objectors aim to
refuse the social expectations compelling them to play a part in maintaining and enhancing militarism. *Davut's* endeavour to clarify that objection
transcends the individual's demand to be exempted from a compulsory
duty reminds us that militaries are not 'pawns and knights to be moved
by uniformed and civilian elites around a chessboard [. . .] militaries are
a lot more fragile and contingent than elites will admit' (Enloe 2015: 8).
Further, the extent to which militaries hide such fragility determines the
level of their legitimacy and public support. Militaries do not occur in a
vacuum. They are the products of an on-going effort (Enloe 2015). One
can read conscientious objection to them as an attempt to distract such
on-going effort and show how fragile the 'normalised' militarism and
the militaries actually are.

Conclusion

As Connell (2005) argues, the path towards demilitarisation and peace
inevitably involves a struggle to transform masculinities. Thus, this
chapter has approached militarism through the eyes of conscientious
objectors, those representing the most dedicated group challenging the
militarisation of everyday life and raising public awareness of the link
between gender and militarism. During the interviews, most of them
referred to gender norms as the underlying reason for their objections
and the normalisation of militarisation. Their critique of masculinity,
heroism and martyrdom and the narratives emerging out of the interviews illustrate that women's rejections have significant impacts on
extending the definition of conscientious objection. Women have used
conscientious objection as a tool to refuse the impacts of militarisation
on their lives and to reject aspects of everyday militarism. Put differently,
since Turkey still adopts the conscription system, the challenges to militarism and gendered practices in everyday life occur particularly through
refusal of compulsory military service. Contrary to the narrow understanding of conscientious objection, which considers objectors' refusal
as only a request for exemption from military service, objectors have

broad motivations, ranging from challenging gender norms to questioning the militarisation of everyday life.

The chapter has shed light particularly on women conscientious objectors' experiences with militarism to expose the workings of militarisation at levels other than the institutional. By carrying women objectors' activism into the academic sphere, it aimed to contribute to their struggle to make sense of their objection within the male conscription system. At the academic level, focusing on female conscientious objectors in Turkey has helped us to include women in our understanding of conscientious objection, whatever their legal obligations as citizens. Therefore, the chapter, with an aim to extend the scope of conscientious objection, has showed that conscientious objection is not only a 'man issue', as militarism infiltrates the lives of people and endows them with an identity that reproduces the core tenets of militarism. Women, even though they are not subject to conscription, are thus an essential part of the conscientious movement in Turkey. Indeed, women's objection has raised public awareness and a set of concerns about the hidden aspects of the militarisation process, thus opening up new lines of enquiry: that is, women and militarism.

Notes

1. In the *Ulke v. Turkey* case, the European Court of Human rights stated that: 'They [repeated prosecutions] are aimed more at repressing the applicant's intellectual personality, inspiring in him feelings of fear, anguish and vulnerability capable of humiliating and debasing him and breaking his resistance and will. The clandestine life, amounting almost to "civil death", which the applicant has been compelled to adopt is incompatible with the punishment regime of a democratic society.' *Ulke v. Turkey* App. No. 39437/98 (ECtHR, 24 April 2004) at [62].
2. *Kişer Pari Mama* means 'Good night, mum' in Armenian. Atlas refers to an Armenian soldier, Sevag Şahin Balıkçı, who died during his compulsory service in Turkey. These were the last few words that his mother, Ani Balıkçı, heard from him.
3. Prime Minister Erdoğan, in a public speech in 2016, expressed the view that women without children are 'incomplete women' (*eksik kadin*). See <http://www.diken.com.tr/erdogan-kadinligin-tanimini-da-yapti-anneligi-reddeden-kadin-eksiktir-yarimdir/> (last accessed 6 January 2022).
4. It should be noted that the chapter focuses on binary gender categories (man/woman) as produced through and productive of militarisation.
5. Yet, though they are a homogeneous group coming from Kurd, Alevi, secular and middle-class families, their family's reaction differs considerably. While some of the participants believe that their family does not understand them, others experience family support or at least they believe that they have made their voice heard.

Conclusion: Demilitarisation of Society

It was a summer's day in 2016. Unaware of my bias and stereotypes, I went to a religious publishing company in Taksim (Istanbul) to interview a religious conscientious objector, *Mehmet*. It was Ramadan and it was hot. On my way there, I finished a bottle of water, assuming that he would be fasting, and it would not be appropriate to drink water in front of someone fasting. When I got there, the scene I had pictured in my mind was proved completely wrong. I found him in a shabby music room, smoking and drinking alcohol. From the first moment of the interview, I understood that his religious identity differed from my own understanding of religion. *Mehmet*'s perspective illustrated how a wide range of motivations and beliefs could lead individuals to declare their conscientious objections, while *Davut* and *Gökhan*, on the legal side, showed me how the law is a vital tool in the struggle of a social movement aiming to bring about change. They revealed once again the necessity to carry the struggle into the legal arena. And, who could forget *Atlas*'s endless energy, *Özlem*'s constructive anger and *Meltem Nur*'s hope for change?

I finished my fieldwork, having regained my faith in the idea that 'change is possible'. All the interviewees revealed that conscientious objectors in Turkey, even though they are few in number, provide an intellectually rich and wide perspective on our militarised world. They challenge the social and historical factors contributing to militarism. They seek to raise awareness of how militaries convince youth to be part of their mechanism. Historically, the military persuaded young people to participate by integrating the concepts of 'nation-in-arms' and 'citizen-soldier' into society. These concepts have preserved their validity in contemporary Turkey with the myth of 'every Turk is born a soldier', constituting the main concern of the conscientious objectors. Objectors aim to challenge these myths and their predetermined roles. Rather than following the roles assigned to them, they want to (re)shape their place in society themselves. They refuse to adhere to socially constructed norms that grant the TAF a strong position and determine the roles of 'good citizens'.

History is evolving. Turkey's constantly changing political atmosphere has had an impact on the public image of TAF and its role in politics. Initially, the 15 July 2016 coup attempt created confusion around the long-established trust in the TAF. The unquestionable was undoubtedly questioned. Yet, this social change did not mark an era of demilitarisation. On the contrary, society needed to take shelter behind more nationalistic concepts. Comments such as 'either you are one of us or a "terrorist"' polarised people. The date, 15 July, has been turned into a 'Day of Democracy' and a celebration of a 'victory' that needed to be honoured. Universities, schools and public institutions organise events to commemorate those who took to the streets that night, the 'martyrs' and 'heroes'. Schools and main streets in almost all the cities of Turkey have, of course, been renamed '15 July Martyrs'. The tendency to construct cultural and racial characteristics with militaristic values – the values that are, actually, the main reason behind the lack of legal recognition of the right to conscientious objection – has continued.

Rejection of socially accepted values comes at a price. Conscientious objectors face human rights violations, despite international and regional documents recognising the right to conscientious objection as it is derived from the right to religion, conscience and thought. Domestic law, incompatible with international standards, criminalises conscientious objection, particularly under Article 318 of the Turkish Penal Code, entitled 'alienating people from military service'. While deciding on cases under Article 318, domestic courts adopt a restrictive understanding of the right to conscientious objection and also narrow the scope of this right. Such a narrow reading limits the claims of conscientious objectors, whose understanding stems from international standards relating to the right to conscientious objection. Explicit legal recognition of the right to conscientious objection is needed to put an end to these human rights abuses. Motivations behind conscientious objection differ considerably, based on whether the objection is religious or non-religious, selective or universal, alternative or absolute. Therefore, the right to conscientious objection needs to cover non-religious objectors (those objecting because of their political and non-religious beliefs), selective objectors (those objecting to a specific war due to their critique of the state's current policies) and absolutist objectors (those who object to completing any alternative form of service, even if it is civil in nature, as their objection not only seeks exemption from the taking up of arms but also demands change in the militarist and gendered implementations).

The conscientious objection movement in Turkey not only requests the recognition of the right to conscientious objection but also challenges the system. The act of objection is related both to preserving the objectors' inner convictions and to changing the social environment, so that they can, indeed, act in accordance with such inner convictions. Further, when they refuse to serve in the military, they make their point via symbolic acts, such as publicly declaring their objection, which mostly involves the act of protesting and burning their draft papers. Their acts aim at gaining the support of members of the public and raising awareness of militarism. Therefore, their objection is a public act like any other act of civil disobedience. Since militarism enjoys a dominant position in society, conscientious objectors in Turkey aim to bring about change in the militarist structure of society rather than confining their objection to military service only. As Nilgun Toker Kılınç (2009: 69–70) illustrates, their reading of militarism objects not only to war, weapons or even the military as an institution, but also to social norms that normalise war and militarism. As a 'regime of obedience', militarism 'subordinates citizens to the will of the state'. In this regard, antimilitarist movements refuse this subordination by publicly demanding freedom. Indeed, women's objection in the male-conscription system is the best indicator that conscientious objection is an act that goes beyond a personal demand for exemption from military service. Their objection has revealed that the gendered understanding within the military impacts the construction of gender stereotypes within the entire society, particularly in highly militarised circles where becoming a soldier is considered the highest virtue (Duncanson 2015: 232).

When becoming a soldier is seen as a sign of becoming a 'real' man and when women are allocated certain roles such as being a 'supportive partner or patriotic mother of a soldier', these gendered norms are no longer intrinsic to the army in particular but also become integrated into society. Therefore, militarisation involves not only soldiers but also women and society at large. For this reason, even though women are not subject to conscription, their objection is accepted as part of the movement. As indicated by Cynthia Cockburn (2013: 446), gender awareness constitutes the major pattern of effectiveness of peace movements' and 'gender relations are deeply implicated in what is done to turn ordinary people into soldiers and shape them up for fighting'. Yet, as argued by

Enloe, 'women and men each can become militarized, though usually they are militarized in rather different ways because militaristic ideas are so deeply imbued with gendered assumptions and values' (Enloe 2007: 11). In other words, the process of militarism affects both men's and women's daily lives in different ways. While men are expected to be always ready to defend their countries, women are also assigned certain roles to play, such as being patriotic mothers or loyal and grateful wives, and getting involved in campaigns compelling men to enlist. Therefore, any antimilitarist movement inevitably involves gender critique.

Notes from Fieldwork

Findings from my fieldwork demonstrate that the most common reference amongst participants is the political and cultural dynamics of the war environment in Turkey. The questions I posed in relation to the typology of their objection were answered by highlighting three major points. The first point was related to the objectors' political views – anarchism and their anti-authoritarian and anti-hierarchic positions. The second point was that they would not serve in any army. The third point was that their rejection includes any service that subjects them to a hierarchy. All these references reveal that their objection is total, absolute and political.

Almost all participants also emphasised that Turkey's social, cultural and political dynamics and the way society perceives military service have significant effects on recognition of the right to conscientious objection and the militarisation of society. In harmony with the findings of Chapter 1, which examines the role of the Turkish army in society, the participants' narratives and attitudes towards social norms revealed that ultimate control of the military is a product of the specific cultural and political structures of Turkey. Participants consistently expressed their desire for changing such norms and linked their claims with peace. This revealed that although the motivations behind the conscientious objectors' act were initially personal, their refusal also involved questioning and challenging the militarisation of society. Since their objection has political implications, it is no longer personal but public. It is clear from the data that such political motivations are followed by the objectors' purpose to engage in public discussion through their non-violent declarations and their willingness to face the consequences of their act. All these references reveal that their objection is an act of civil disobedience.

Another common point among participants was their direct reference to gender norms as an underlying reason for their objections and the normalisation of militarisation. The objectors' critique of masculinity, heroism and martyrdom and the narratives emerging out of the interviews also illustrate that women's rejections have a great impact on extending the definition of conscientious objection. Women were able to enlarge the scope of conscientious objection, thus achieving a feminist efficacy in direct opposition to the militarisation process. That is to say, women used conscientious objection as a tool to refuse the impacts of militarisation on their lives and also to reject aspects of everyday militarism. This, of course, cannot only be seen in reference to the army but is also an overarching critique of the present political situation in Turkey. Indeed, women's objection has raised public awareness and a set of concerns about the hidden aspects of the militarisation process and also opened up new lines of enquiry relating to women and war, which the academic elite consider worthy of detailed examination.

To sum up, it is evident from the interview data that the objection movement in Turkey does not just refuse the duty of compulsory military service. It instead aims to challenge the sociological elements that maintain the conscription system. Conscientious objectors, both women and men, are asking for societal change. They reject not only a duty but also the gendered and militarised system that maintains conscription and, as such, influences the entire society. In this sense, their objection is both individual and political.

Further Research

Since Turkey still adopts conscription and has a prominent military history, it constitutes a stimulating case for examining the impacts of society's cultural characteristics on recognition of the right to conscientious objection in order to offer a socio-legal study. Even though conscientious objection has attracted some attention in the academy, it still cannot be debated publicly and in academic arenas in Turkey. Discussions on conscientious objection mostly remain within the alternative media because studies are limited. Further research is needed to bring the conscientious objection movement to both academic and public attention, and to open debates in both spheres to raise awareness on the subject, break taboos and touch on an issue that remains unchallenged. This book has engaged with major research questions and provided a nuanced understanding of conscientious objection, yet it did not broach several issues. It is essential to point out the possible niches for further studies.

On the empirical side, the book has focused only on active conscientious objectors, those who object mostly because of their anarchist views. Although interviewing objectors, those who constitute the marginalised group, was vital to understanding the major reasons for refusal, conducting interviews with mothers of martyrs and soldiers remains essential to the study of militarism in society. On the theoretical side, the book has primarily focused on the link between gender roles and the militarisation of society. However, it is important to scrutinise the role of nationalism in relation to recognition of the right to conscientious objection. Furthermore, to explore the gendered dimensions of military service, the book has focused only on the exclusion of women from such a duty. Since women's active role in the military cannot be considered as a sign of less militarised–masculine societies, the main aim was not to include women in the army but to demonstrate how perceiving women as 'the protected' and men as 'the protectors' has helped the authorities to maintain the system.

The number of women in the military has been increasing, particularly in the US, but militaries in most countries are still male-dominated institutions. Furthermore, even in states where both women and men are subject to compulsory military service, women, as opposed to men, are not allowed to perform combat duties. Even when they are included in the military, women face discrimination and sexual harassment. Although it is important to consider women's experiences in male-dominated institutions, it is beyond the scope of the present book to study women inside the military. Therefore, further comparative studies on women inside the military and the exclusion of women from military service are necessary. For example, the Israel Defence Forces (IDF), which conscript women, could be one of a series of case studies to illustrate that including women in the army does not provide a less gendered army, and can also afford a picture of gendered implementations within the military.

This book intentionally limits itself to investigating resistance to compulsory military service as an objection to militarism and gender roles during 'peacetime'. Therefore, it focuses on absolute and total conscientious objectors. Although Chapter 4 provides a brief analysis of selective objection and highlights the importance of including selective objection in the definition of conscientious objection, a detailed analysis of selective objection remains essential. The IDF, for instance, could be an ideal area of study to compare absolute objection in Turkey with selective objection which rejects the occupation of Palestine. Further, a detailed analysis of alternativist conscientious objection would allow the assessment of a possible change in Turkey. The questions that Chapter 4 raised merit further examination. The most prominent ones include: who should administer the alternative civilian service? What sort of alternative service is acceptable? In this sense, Germany, which initially recognised conscientious objection with an alternative service but later abolished conscription, could be a potential case for examining the advantages and disadvantages of recognising conscientious objection with an alternative civil service. This would provide insights into the question of whether recognition of the right to conscientious objection provides a solution to the problems associated with the lack of explicit recognition of the right to conscientious objection in Turkey. In line with that, Germany as a case study would also offer insights for evaluating the potential legal reforms regarding recognition of the right to conscientious objection in Turkey.

The limitations of this book could be considered as a potential site for future work on comparative studies which examine the conscription systems and recognition of the right to conscientious objection in other militaries, such as the German army and the IDF. In other words, the book has contributed to central issues of social science such as antimilitarism and gender studies. However, comparative research that includes multiple case studies and a detailed examination of social movements around forced recruitment are needed. Such case studies that consider many significant contextual and historical factors will offer a comprehensive understanding of why the particular recognition of the right to conscientious objection occurred as it did and whether this can be applied to the case of Turkey. Therefore, further study is required to add to the literature a comparative analysis of the right to conscientious objection in Turkey.

Hope for Change? Final Suggestions for Potential Legal Reforms

Drawing on the interview findings, the book suggests two main recommendations for possible legal reforms in Turkey. Regarding the first recommendation, some reforms could be made to the current legal system, which subjects objectors to a 'fear' of repeated convictions. The abolition of Article 318 of the Turkish Penal Code is necessary to protect objectors and their supporters from the risk of prosecution. As for the second recommendation, an explicit recognition of the right to conscientious objection should be granted. The findings of the interviews with conscientious objectors illustrated that conscientious objection in Turkey stems from the objector's political and humanitarian views. Given the typology of objection in Turkey, which is total and political, introducing a law that recognises ethical, humanitarian, philosophical and political beliefs as legitimate grounds for objection is necessary. Such a reform would also be compatible with both the wording and the spirit of the

Turkish Constitution, which protects the right to freedom of conscience. Furthermore, most objectors are absolute objectors, which means they will not cooperate with any reform that requires an alternative form of service. Since most objectors are absolutists who reject any form of service, an alternative service that is non-punitive and civil may be a solution , but only for those who are eager to cooperate. The absolutist objectors, however, will continue to object to the alternative service. It is important to clarify that in the case of an explicit and inclusive recognition of the right to conscientious objection that includes absolute, total and political forms of objection, the legal aspects of the matter will be solved, yet objectors will keep resisting gendered and militarist structures in other ways. That is to say, legal recognition is required to bring an end to human rights violations, yet demilitarisation can be achieved via changing the social norms empowering militarism.

BIBLIOGRAPHY

Açıksöz, Salih Caan. 2017. 'He Is a Lynched Soldier Now: Coup, Militarism, and Masculinity in Turkey'. *Journal of Middle East Women's Studies* 13 (1): 178–80. <https://doi.org/10.1215/15525864-3728811> (last accessed 3 January 2022).

Ahdar, Rex, and Ian Leigh. 2005. *Religious Freedom in the Liberal State*. Oxford: Oxford University Press.

Aknur, Müge. 2012. 'The Impact of Civil-Military Relations on Democratic Consolidation in Turkey'. In *Democratic Consolidation in Turkey*, edited by Müge Aknur, 203–48. Boca Raton: Universal-Publishers.

Aktas, Fatma Oya. 2014. *Being a Conscientious Objector in Turkey: Challenging Hegemonic Masculinity in a Militaristic Nation-State*. Saarbrücken: LAP LAMBERT Academic Publishing.

Allan, T. R. S. 1996. 'Citizenship and Obligation: Civil Disobedience and Civil Dissent'. *The Cambridge Law Journal* 55 (01): 89. <https://doi.org/10.1017/S0008197300097750> (last accessed 3 January 2022).

Altınay, Ayşe Gül. 2004. *The Myth of the Military Nation: Militarism, Gender, and Education in Turkey*. New York: Palgrave Macmillan.

Altinay, Ayse Gül. 2009. 'Refusing to Identify as Obedient Wives, Sacrificing Mothers and Proud Warriors'. In *Conscientious Objection: Resisting Militarized Society*, edited by Özgür Heval Çınar and Coşkun Üsterci, 88–105. New York and London: Zed Books.

Arslan, Atlas. 2015. *Kişer Pari Mama: Kadınlar Savaşı Reddediyor (Women Are Rejecting War)*. Ankara: Phoenix.

Article 19 and Liberty, ed. 2000. *Secrets, Spies and Whistleblowers: Freedom of Expression and National Security in the United Kingdom*. London: Article 19 and Liberty.

Asal, Victor, Justin Conrad and Nathan Toronto. 2017. 'I Want You! The Determinants of Military Conscription'. *Journal of Conflict Resolution* 61 (7): 1456–81. <https://doi.org/10.1177/0022002715606217> (last accessed 3 January 2022).

Asbjern, Eide, and Mubanga-Chipoya Chama/United Nations. 1985. 'Conscientious Objection to Military Service, 1985, E/CN.4/Sub.2/1983/30/Rev.1'. <https://www.refworld.org/docid/5107cd132.html> (last accessed 18 January 2022).

Aviram, Hadar. 2015. 'Book Review: The Right to Conscientious Objection to Military Service and Turkey's Obligations under International Human Rights Law by Ozgur Heval Cinar'. <https://critcom.councilforeuropeanstudies.org/the-right-to-conscientious-objection-to-military-service-and-turkeys-obligations-under-international-human-rights-law/> (last accessed 10 October 2016).

Aydinli, Ersel. 2009. 'A Paradigmatic Shift for the Turkish Generals and an End to the Coup Era in Turkey'. *The Middle East Journal* 63 (4): 581–96.

Aydinli, Ersel, Nihat Ali Ozcan and Dogan Akyaz. 2006. 'The Turkish Military's March toward Europe'. *Foreign Affairs* 85: 77.

Aydinli, Ersel, and Dov Waxman. 2001. 'A Dream Become Nightmare? Turkey's Entry into the European Union'. *Current History* 100 (649): 381.

Aydın, Suavi. 2009. 'The Militarization of Society: Conscription and National Armies in the Process of Citizen Creation'. In *Conscientious Objection: Resisting Militarized Society*, edited by Özgür Heval Çınar and Coşkun Üsterci, 17–36. New York and London: Zed Books.

Başdaş, Begüm. 2017. 'Unity in Rupture: Women against the Coup Attempt in Turkey'. *Journal of Middle East Women's Studies* 13 (1): 186–8. <https://doi.org/10.1215/15525864-3728833> (last accessed 3 January 2022).

Basham, Victoria M. 2015. 'Gender, Race, Militarism and Remembrance: The Everyday Geopolitics of the Poppy'. *Gender, Place & Culture*, October, 1–14. <https://doi.org/10.1080/0966369X.2015.1090406> (last accessed 3 January 2022).

Bedau, Hugo Adam. 1961. 'On Civil Disobedience'. *The Journal of Philosophy* 58 (21): 653. <https://doi.org/10.2307/2023542> (last accessed 3 January 2022).

Bedau, Hugo Adam. 1991. 'Civil Disobedience and Personal Responsibility for Injustice'. In *Civil Disobedience in Focus*, edited by Hugo Adam Bedau. London and New York: Routledge.

Belkin, A. 2003. 'Don't Ask, Don't Tell: Is the Gay Ban Based on Military Necessity?' *Parameters : Journal of the US Army War College* 33: 108–19.

Bibbings, Lois. 2003. 'Images of Manliness: The Portrayal of Soldiers and Conscientious Objectors in the Great War'. *Social & Legal Studies* 12 (3): 335–58.

Bilgin, Pinar. 2005. 'Turkey's Changing Security Discourses: The Challenge of Globalisation'. *European Journal of Political Research* 44 (1): 175–201.

Bilgin, Pınar. 2007. 'Making Turkey's Transformation Possible: Claiming "Security-Speak" – Not Desecuritization!' *Southeast European and Black Sea Studies* 7 (4): 555–71.

Biricik, Alp. 2009. 'Rotten Report and Reconstructing Hegemonic Masculinity in Turkey'. In *Don't Ask, Don't Tell: Is the Gay Ban Based on Military Necessity?*, edited by Özgür Heval Çınar and Coşkun Üsterci. New York and London: Zed Books.

Blanton, Shannon Lindsey. 1999. 'Instruments of Security or Tools of Repression? Arms Imports and Human Rights Conditions in Developing Countries'. *Journal of Peace Research* 36 (2): 233–44.

Bloom, Harold. 2002. *Poets of World War I: Wilfred Owen & Isaac Rosenberg*. Broomall, PA: Chelsea House.

Boyle, Kevin. 2009. 'Conscientious Objection in International Law and the Osman Murat Ulke Case'. In *Conscientious Objection: Resisting Militarized Society*, edited by Özgür Heval Çınar and Coşkun Üsterci, 212–27. New York and London: Zed Books.

Brett, Rachel, and Laurel Townhead. 2011. 'Conscientious Objection to Military Service'. *Strategic Visions for Human Rights: Essays in Honour of Professor Kevin Boyle*, 91–107. London: Routledge.

Bröckling, Ulrich. 2009. 'Sand in the Wheels? Conscientious Objection at the Turn of the Twenty-first Century'. In *Conscientious Objection: Resisting Militarized Society*, edited by Özgür Heval Çınar and Coşkun Üsterci, 53–60. New York and London: Zed Books.

Brownlee, Kimberley. 2004. 'Features of a Paradigm Case of Civil Disobedience'. *Res Publica: A Journal of Legal and Social Philosophy* 10 (4): 337–51.

Brownlee, Kimberley. 2012. 'Conscientious Objection and Civil Disobedience'. Social Science Research Network. <http://papers.ssrn.com/abstract=2091045> (last accessed 3 January 2022).

Brownlee, Kimberley. 2016. 'The Civil Disobedience of Edward Snowden: A Reply to William Scheuerman'. *Philosophy & Social Criticism* 42 (10): 965–70. <https://doi.org/10.1177/0191453716631167> (last accessed 3 January 2022).

Burk, James. 1992. 'The Decline of Mass Armed Forces and Compulsory Military Service'. *Defense Analysis* 8 (1): 45–59.

Burk, James. 1995. 'Citizenship Status and Military Service: The Quest for Inclusion by Minorities and Conscientious Objectors'. *Armed Forces & Society* 21 (4): 503–29. <https://doi.org/10.1177/0095327X9502100401> (last accessed 3 January 2022).

Caliskan, Koray. 2017. 'Explaining the End of Military Tutelary Regime and the July 15 Coup Attempt in Turkey'. *Journal of Cultural Economy* 10 (1): 97–111. <https://doi.org/10.1080/17530350.2016.1260628> (last accessed 3 January 2022).

Caltekin, Demet Asli. 2018. 'Can We Reverse Militarism? The Politics of Demilitarisation in Turkey'. *Critical Military Studies*, October, 1–4. <https://doi.org/10.1080/23337486.2018.1521602> (last accessed 3 January 2022).

Campbell Public Affairs Institute, ed. 2003. *National Security and Open Government: Striking the Right Balance*. New York: Maxwell School of Syracuse University.

Can, Osman. 2009. 'Conscientious Objection and the Turkish Constitution'. In *Conscientious Objection: Resisting Militarized Society*, edited by Özgür Heval Çınar and Coşkun Üsterci, 227–42. New York and London: Zed Books.

Carden-Coyne, Ana. 2012. 'Introduction: Gender and Conflict Since 1914: Historical and Interdisciplinary Perspectives'. In *Gender and Conflict Since 1914: Historical and Interdisciplinary Perspectives*, edited by Ana Carden-Coyne. Basingstoke: Palgrave Macmillan.

Celenk, Ayse Aslıhan. 2009. 'Democratization of the National Security Discourse and the Political Parties in Turkey'. *Erciyes Üniversitesi İktisadi ve İdari Bilimler Fakültesi Dergisi* 33: 119–34.

Celikates, Robin. 2016. 'Democratizing Civil Disobedience'. *Philosophy & Social Criticism* 42 (10): 982–94. <https://doi.org/10.1177/0191453716638562> (last accessed 3 January 2022).

Charlesworth, Hilary. 2008. 'Are Women Peaceful? Reflections on the Role of Women in Peace-Building'. *Feminist Legal Studies* 16 (3): 347–61. <https://doi.org/10.1007/s10691-008-9101-6> (last accessed 3 January 2022).

Choulis, Ioannis, Zorzeta Bakaki and Tobias Böhmelt. 2019. 'Public Support for the Armed Forces: The Role of Conscription'. *Defence and Peace Economics*, December, 1–12. <https://doi.org/10.1080/10242694.2019.1709031> (last accessed 3 January 2022).

Cinar, Ozgur Heval. 2013. *Conscientious Objection to Military Service in International Human Rights Law*. Basingstoke: Palgrave Macmillan.

Cizre, Umit. 2004. 'Problems of Democratic Governance of Civil-Military Relations in Turkey and the European Union Enlargement Zone'. *European Journal of Political Research* 43 (1): 107–25.

Cizre, Umit. 2007. *Prime Movers, Specific Features and Challenges of Security Sector Reform in a 'Guardian State': The Case of Turkey*. Geneva: Geneva Centre for the Democratic Control of Armed Forces (DCAF).

Cizre, Umit. 2011. 'Disentangling the Threads of Civil-Military Relations in Turkey: Promises and Perils'. *Mediterranean Quarterly* 22 (2): 57–75. <https://doi.org/10.1215/10474552-1263397> (last accessed 3 January 2022).

Çınar, Özgür Heval. 2013. *Conscientious Objection to Military Service in International Human Rights Law*. Basingstoke: Palgrave Macmillan.

Çınar, Özgür Heval. 2014. *The Right to Conscientious Objection to Military Service and Turkey's Obligations under International Human Rights Law*. Basingstoke: Palgrave Macmillan.

Çınar, Özgür Heval, and Coşkun Üsterci, eds. 2009a. *Conscientious Objection: Resisting Militarized Society*. New York and London: Zed Books.

Çınar, Özgür Heval, and Coşkun Üsterci. 2009b. 'Introduction'. In *Conscientious Objection: Resisting Militarized Society*, edited by Özgür Heval Çınar and Coşkun Üsterci. New York and London: Zed Books.

Clifford, George. 2011. 'Legalizing Selective Conscientious Objection'. *Public Reason* 3 (1).

Coady, C. A. J. 1997. 'Objecting Morally'. *The Journal of Ethics* 1 (4): 375–97.

Cockburn, Cynthia. 2010. 'Gender Relations as Causal in Militarization and War'. *International Feminist Journal of Politics* 12 (2): 139–57. <https://doi.org/10.1080/14616741003665169> (last accessed 3 January 2022).

Cockburn, Cynthia. 2013. 'War and Security, Women and Gender: An Overview of the Issues'. *Gender & Development* 21 (3): 433–52. <https://doi.org/10.1080/13552074.2013.846632> (last accessed 3 January 2022).

Cockburn, Cynthia, and Dubravka Žarkov. 2002. *The Postwar Moment: Militaries, Masculinities and International Peacekeeping, Bosnia and the Netherlands*. London: Lawrence & Wishart.

Cohen, Carl. 1966. 'Civil Disobedience and the Law'. *Rutgers Law Review* 21: 1.

Cohen, Carl. 1968. 'Conscientious Objection'. *Ethics* 78 (4): 269–79.

Cohen, David M., and Robert Greenspan. 1967. 'Conscientious Objection, Democratic Theory, and the Constitution'. *University of Pittsburgh Law Review* 29: 389.

Coliver, Sandra, ed. 1999. *Secrecy and Liberty: National Security, Freedom of Expression, and Access to Information*. International Studies in Human Rights, vol. 58. Leiden: M. Nijhoff.

Connell, R. W. 2005. *Masculinities*. 2nd edn. Berkeley: University of California Press.

Cooke, Maeve, and Danielle Petherbridge. 2016. 'Civil Disobedience and Conscientious Objection'. *Philosophy & Social Criticism* 42 (10): 953–7. <https://doi.org/10.1177/0191453716659522> (last accessed 3 January 2022).

Council of Europe: Committee of Ministers. 1987. 'Recommendation No. R (87) 8 of the Committee of Ministers to Member States Regarding Conscientious Objection to Compulsory Military Service'. <http://www.refworld.org/docid/5069778e2.html> (last accessed 3 January 2022).

Cumper, Peter. 2001. 'The Public Manifestation of Religion or Belief: Challenges for a Multi-Faith Society in the Twenty-first Century'. In *Law and Religion*, edited by Andrew Lewis and Richard O'Dair. Current Legal Issues. Oxford: Oxford University Press.

Decker, D. Christopher, and Lucia Fresa. 2000. 'The Status of Conscientious Objection under Article 4 of the European Convention on Human Rights'. *New York University Journal of International Law and Politics* 33: 379.

Demirel, Tanel. 2004. 'Soldiers and Civilians: The Dilemma of Turkish Democracy'. *Middle Eastern Studies* 40 (1): 127–50.

Denscombe, Martyn. 2003. *The Good Research Guide: For Small-Scale Social Research Projects*. 2nd edn. Maidenhead and New York: Open University Press.

Denscombe, Martyn. 2010. *The Good Research Guide for Small-Scale Social Research Projects*. Maidenhead and New York: McGraw-Hill/Open University Press.

Donnici, Peter J. 1964. 'Government Encouragement of Religious Ideology: A Study of the Current Conscientious Objector Exemption from Military Service'. *Journal of Public Law* 13: 16.

Doorn, Jacques van. 1975. 'The Decline of the Mass Army in the West General Reflections'. *Armed Forces & Society* 1 (2): 147–57. <https://doi.org/10.1177/0095327X7500100201> (last accessed 3 January 2022).

Dowd, Nancy E., Nancy Levit and Ann C. McGinley. 2011. 'Feminist Legal Theory Meets Masculinities Theory'. In *Masculinities and Law: A Multidimensional Approach*, edited by Frank Rudy Cooper and Ann C. McGinley. New York: New York University Press.

Duncanson, Claire. 2015. 'Hegemonic Masculinity and the Possibility of Change in Gender Relations'. *Men and Masculinities* 18 (2): 231–48. <https://doi.org/10.1177/1097184X15584912> (last accessed 3 January 2022).

Dworkin, Ronald. 1977. *Taking Rights Seriously*. London: Duckworth.

Edel, Frédéric. 2010. *The Prohibition of Discrimination under the European Convention on Human Rights*. Strasbourg: Council of Europe.

Edge, Peter W. 1996. 'Current Problems in Article 9 of the European Convention on Human Rights'. *The Juridical Review* 1: 42–50.

Eide, Asbjørn, and Chama Mubanga-Chipoya/United Nations. 1985. 'Conscientious Objection to Military Service', E/CN.4/Sub.2/1983/30/Rev.1. <https://www.refworld.org/docid/5107cd132.html> (last accessed 18 January 2022).

Einstein, Albert. 2010. *The Ultimate Quotable Einstein*. Princeton: Princeton University Press.

Enloe, Cynthia. 1988. *Does Khaki Become You?: The Militarization of Women's Lives*. London: Pandora.

Enloe, Cynthia. 2004. *The Curious Feminist: Searching for Women in a New Age of Empire*. Berkeley: University of California Press.

Enloe, Cynthia. 2007. *Globalization and Militarism: Feminists Make the Link*. Lanham, MD: Rowman & Littlefield.

Enloe, Cynthia. 2009. 'Where Are the Women in Military Conscientious Objection? Some Feminist Clues'. In *Conscientious Objection: Resisting Militarized Society*, edited by Özgür Heval Çınar and Coşkun Üsterci. New York and London: Zed Books.

Enloe, Cynthia. 2015. 'The Recruiter and the Sceptic: A Critical Feminist Approach to Military Studies'. *Critical Military Studies* 1 (1): 3–10. <https://doi.org/10.1080/23337486.2014.961746> (last accessed 3 January 2022).

Enloe, Cynthia. 2016. *Globalization and Militarism: Feminists Make the Link*. Lanham, MD: Rowman & Littlefield.

Evans, Carolyn. 2003. *Freedom of Religion under the European Convention on Human Rights*. Oxford ECHR Series. Oxford: Oxford University Press.

Evans, Malcolm D. 2001. 'Human Rights, Religious Liberty, and the Universality Debate'. In *Law and Religion*, edited by Richard O'Dair and Andrew Lewis. Current Legal Issues. Oxford: Oxford University Press.

Evans, Malcolm D. 2008a. 'Freedom of Religion and the European Convention on Human Rights: Approaches, Trends and Tensions'. In *Law and Religion in*

Theoretical and Historical Context, edited by Peter Cane, Carolyn Evans and Zoë Robinson, 291–315. Cambridge: Cambridge University Press.

Evans, Malcolm D. 2008b. *Religious Liberty and International Law in Europe*. Cambridge: Cambridge University Press.

Flauss, Jean-François. 2009. 'The European Court of Human Rights and the Freedom of Expression'. *Indiana Law Journal* 84 (3).

Frevert, Ute. 2004. *A Nation in Barracks: Modern Germany, Military Conscription and Civil Society*. Oxford: Berg.

Gilbert, Howard. 2001. 'The Slow Development of the Right to Conscientious Objection to Military Service under the European Convention on Human Rights'. *European Human Rights Law Review* 5, 554–67.

Golan, Galia. 1997. 'Militarization and Gender: The Israeli Experience'. *Women's Studies International Forum*, Cultures of Womanhood in Israel, 20 (5–6): 581–6. <https://doi.org/10.1016/S0277-5395(97)00063-0> (last accessed 3 January 2022).

Goldstein, Joshua S. 2003. *War and Gender: How Gender Shapes the War System and Vice Versa*. Cambridge: Cambridge University Press.

Greenawalt, Kent. 1991. 'Justifying Nonviolent Disobedience'. In *Civil Disobedience in Focus*, edited by Hugo Adam Bedau. London and New York: Routledge.

Griggs, Walter S. 1979. 'The Selective Conscientious Objector: A Vietnam Legacy'. *Journal of Church and State* 21 (1): 91–107. <https://doi.org/10.1093/jcs/21.1.91> (last accessed 3 January 2022).

Hammer, Leonard M. 2001. *The International Human Right to Freedom of Conscience: Some Suggestions for Its Development and Application*. Aldershot: Ashgate.

Hammer, Leonard. 2002. 'Selective Conscientious Objection and International Human Rights'. *Israel Law Review* 36: 145.

Haraszti, Miklos. 2005. 'Review of the Draft Turkish Penal Code: Freedom of Media Concerns'. Representative on Freedom of the Media, OSCE, Vienna, May. <http://www.osce.org/fom/14672> (last accessed 24 January 2022).

Harrell, Margaret C., and Melissa Bradley. 2009. *Data Collection Methods: Semi-structured Interviews and Focus Groups*. RAND Corporation Technical Report Series, TR-718-USG. Santa Monica, CA: RAND.

Harris, David John, Michael O'Boyle, Edward Bates, Colin Warbrick and Carla Buckley. 2009. *Law of the European Convention on Human Rights*. 2nd edn. Oxford: Oxford University Press.

Harris, George S. 1965. 'The Role of the Military in Turkish Politics'. *Middle East Journal* 19 (1): 54–66.

Harris, George S. 1988. 'The Role of the Military in Turkey in the 1980s: Guardians or Decision-Makers?' In *State, Democracy, and the Military*, edited by Metin Heper and Ahmet Evin. Berlin: De Gruyter.

Huntington, Samuel P. 1957. *The Soldier and the State: The Theory and Politics of Civil-Military Relations*. Cambridge, MA: Harvard University Press.

Jenkins, Gareth. 2007. 'Continuity and Change: Prospects for Civil–Military Relations in Turkey'. *International Affairs* 83 (2): 339–55.

Karaca, Ekin. 2012. 'Milestone Decision for Conscientious Objection in Turkey'. Bianet – Bagimsiz Iletisim Agi. <http://www.bianet.org/english/religion/136857-milestone-decision-for-conscientious-objection-in-turkey> (last accessed 3 January 2022).

Kaufman, Arnold S. 1968. 'The Selective Service System: Actualities and Alternatives'. In *A Conflict of Loyalties: The Case for Selective Conscientious Objection*, edited by James Finn, 240. New York: Pegasus.

Kessler, Jeremy K. 2013. 'The Invention of a Human Right: Conscientious Objection at the United Nations, 1947–2011'. *Columbia Human Rights Law Review* 44 (3): 753–91.

Keyman, Ariana. 2012. 'Civil-Military Relations in Turkey'. *E-International Relations* (blog). <http://www.e-ir.info/2012/05/21/civil-military-relations-in-turkey/> (last accessed 3 January 2022).

Kovitz, Marcia. 2003. 'The Roots of Military Masculinity'. In *Military Masculinities: Identity and the State*, edited by Paul Higate. Westport, CT: Praeger.

Krebs, Ronald R. 2006. *Fighting for Rights: Military Service and the Politics of Citizenship*. Ithaca, NY: Cornell University Press.

Kumar, Deepa. 2004. 'War Propaganda and the (AB)Uses of Women: Media Constructions of the Jessica Lynch Story'. *Feminist Media Studies* 4 (3): 297–313. <https://doi.org/10.1080/1468077042000309955> (last accessed 3 January 2022).

Leigh, Ian. 2012. 'Religious Freedom in the UK after the Human Rights Act 1998.' In *Freedom of Religion Under Bills of Rights*. Adelaide: University of Adelaide Press. <http://dro.dur.ac.uk/8719/1/8719.pdf> (last accessed 3 January 2022).

Leigh, Ian, and Hans Born. 2008. *Handbook on Human Rights and Fundamental Freedoms of Armed Forces Personnel*. Warsaw: OSCE Office for Democratic Institutions and Human Rights (ODIHR).

Leigh, Ian, and Andrew Hambler. 2014. 'Religious Symbols, Conscience, and the Rights of Others'. *Oxford Journal of Law and Religion* 3 (1): 2–24. <https://doi.org/10.1093/ojlr/rwt048> (last accessed 3 January 2022).

Lerner, Natan. 2006. *Religion, Secular Beliefs and Human Rights: 25 Years After the 1981 Declaration*. Leiden and Boston: M. Nijhoff.

Levi, Margaret. 1997. *Consent, Dissent, and Patriotism*. Cambridge: Cambridge University Press.

Lippman, Matthew. 1990. 'Recognition of Conscientious Objection to Military Service as an International Human Right'. *California Western International Law Journal* 21: 31.

Lubell, Noam. 2002. 'Selective Conscientious Objection in International Law: Refusing to Participate in a Specific Armed Conflict'. *Netherlands Quarterly of Human Rights* 20 (4): 407–22.

Lustgarten, Laurence, and Ian Leigh. 1994. *In from the Cold: National Security and Parliamentary Democracy.* Oxford: Clarendon Press / Oxford University Press.

Lutz, Ralph Haswell. 1933. 'Studies of World War Propaganda, 1914-33'. *The Journal of Modern History* 5 (4): 496–516.

MacGuigan, Mark R. 1971. 'Democracy and Civil Disobedience'. *Canadian Bar Review* 49: 222.

Major, Marie-France. 1992. 'Conscientious Objection and International Law: A Human Right'. *Case Western Reserve Journal of International Law* 24: 349.

Major, Marie-France. 2001. 'Conscientious Objection to Military Service: The European Commission on Human Rights and the Human Rights Committee'. *California Western International Law Journal* 32: 1.

Marcus, Emily N. 1997. 'Conscientious Objection as an Emerging Human Right'. *Virginia Journal of International Law* 38: 507.

Martínez-Torrón, Javier. 2001. 'European Court of Human Rights and Religion'. In *Law and Religion*, edited by Richard O'Dair and Andrew Lewis. Oxford: Oxford University Press.

Mellors, Colin, and John McKean. 1984. 'The Politics of Conscription in Western Europe'. *West European Politics* 7 (3): 25–42.

Momayezi, Nasser. 1998. 'Civil-Military Relations in Turkey'. *International Journal on World Peace* 15 (3): 3–28.

Moon, Seungsook. 2005. 'Trouble with Conscription, Entertaining Soldiers: Popular Culture and the Politics of Militarized Masculinity in South Korea'. *Men and Masculinities* 8 (1): 64–92. <https://doi.org/10.1177/1097184X04268800> (last accessed 3 January 2021).

Morreall, John. 1991. 'The Justifiability of Violent Civil Disobedience'. In *Civil Disobedience in Focus*, edited by Hugo Adam Bedau. London and New York: Routledge.

Moskos, Charles C., and John Whiteclay Chambers II. 1993a. 'Conclusion: The Secularization of Conscience Reconsidered'. In *The New Conscientious Objection: From Sacred to Secular Resistance*, edited by Charles C. Moskos and John Whiteclay Chambers II, 196–208. Oxford: Oxford University Press.

Moskos, Charles C., and John Whiteclay Chambers II, eds. 1993b. *The New Conscientious Objection: From Sacred to Secular Resistance.* Oxford: Oxford University Press.

Moskos, Charles C., and John Whiteclay Chambers II. 1993c. 'The Secularization of Conscience'. In *The New Conscientious Objection: From Sacred to Secular Resistance*, edited by Charles C. Moskos and John Whiteclay Chambers II. Oxford: Oxford University Press.

Muzny, Petr. 2012. '*Bayatyan v Armenia*: The Grand Chamber Renders a Grand Judgment'. *Human Rights Law Review* 12 (1): 135–47. <https://doi.org/10.1093/hrlr/ngr050> (last accessed 3 January 2022).

Nagel, Joane. 1998. 'Masculinity and Nationalism: Gender and Sexuality in the Making of Nations'. *Ethnic and Racial Studies* 21 (2): 242–69. <https://doi.org/10.1080/014198798330007> (last accessed 3 January 2022).

Narli, Nilufer. 2005. 'Aligning Civil-Military Relations in Turkey: Transparency Building in Defence Sector and the EU Reforms'. <https://www.bundesheer.at/pdf_pool/publikationen/10_wg9_taf_110.pdf> (last accessed 24 January 2022).

Narli, Nilufer. 2009a. 'Changes in the Turkish Security Culture and in the Civil-Military Relations'. *Western Balkans Security Observer - English Edition* 14: 56–83.

Narli, Nilufer. 2009b. 'EU Harmonisation Reforms, Democratisation and a New Modality of Civil-Military Relations in Turkey'. In *Contributions to Conflict Management, Peace Economics and Development*, edited by Giuseppe Caforio, 12: 433–72. Bingley: Emerald Group. <https://doi.org/10.1108/S1572-8323(2009)000012B023> (last accessed 3 January 2022).

Noone, Michael. 1993. 'Legal Aspects of Conscientious Objection: A Comparative Analysis'. In *The New Conscientious Objection: From Sacred to Secular Resistance*, edited by Charles C. Moskos and John Whiteclay Chambers II. Oxford: Oxford University Press.

Öztan, Güven Gürkan. 2018. *Türkiye'de militarizm. Zihniyet, pratik, propaganda (Militarism in Turkey: mentality, Practice, and Propaganda)*. Istanbul: Ayrıntı Publishing.

Peterson, V. Spike. 1999. 'Sexing Political Identities/Nationalism as Heterosexism'. *International Feminist Journal of Politics* 1 (1): 34–65. <https://doi.org/10.1080/146167499360031> (last accessed 3 January 2022).

Poutvaara, Panu, and Andreas Wagener. 2007. 'Conscription: Economic Costs and Political Allure'. *The Economics of Peace and Security Journal* 2 (1): 6–15.

Poutvaara, Panu, and Andreas Wagener. 2009. 'The Political Economy of Conscription'. Social Science Research Network. <http://papers.ssrn.com/sol3/papers.cfm?abstract_id=1491419> (last accessed 3 January 2022).

Rawls, John. 1999. *A Theory of Justice*. Cambridge, MA: Belknap Press of Harvard University Press.

Raz, Joseph. 1979. *The Authority of Law: Essays on Law and Morality*. Oxford: Clarendon Press/ Oxford University Press.

Ritchie, Jane, ed. 2011. *Qualitative Research Practice: A Guide for Social Science Students and Researchers*. Repr. Los Angeles: SAGE.

Sagi, Avi, and Ron Shapira. 2002. 'Civil Disobedience and Conscientious Objection'. *Israel Law Review* 36 (Special Issue: Refusals to Serve - Political Dissent in the Israel Defense Forces 03): 181–217. <https://doi.org/10.1017/S0021223700018021> (last accessed 3 January 2022).

Sakallioğlu, Ümit Cizre. 1997. 'The Anatomy of the Turkish Military's Political Autonomy'. *Comparative Politics* 29 (2): 151–66.

Savda, Halil. 2010. 'Halkı Askerlikten Soğutma: 318 Davasında 4 Kişiye Hapis Cezası [Alienating People from Military Service: 4 People Sentenced to Prison in the Article 318 Case]'. *Anarşist Faaliyet* (blog). <http://anarsistfaaliyet.org/sokak/halki-askerlikten-sogutma-318-davasinda-4-kisiye-hapis-cezasi/> (last accessed 3 January 2022).

Scanlon, Thomas. 2003. *The Difficulty of Tolerance: Essays in Political Philosophy*. Cambridge: Cambridge University Press.

Shover, Michele J. 1975. 'Roles and Images of Women in World War I Propaganda'. *Politics & Society* 5 (4): 469–86.

Singer, Peter. 1991. 'Disobedience as a Plea for Reconsideration'. In *Civil Disobedience in Focus*, edited by Hugo Adam Bedau. London and New York: Routledge.

Sjoberg, Laura, and Sandra Via. 2010. 'Introduction'. In *Gender, War, and Militarism: Feminist Perspectives*, edited by Laura Sjoberg and Sandra Via. Santa Barbara, CA: ABC-CLIO.

Skjelsbaek, Kjell. 1979. 'Militarism, its Dimensions and Corollaries: An Attempt at Conceptual Clarification'. *Journal of Peace Research* 16 (3): 213–29.

Smart, Brian, and Hugo Adam Bedau. 1991. 'Defining Civil Disobedience'. In *Civil Disobedience in Focus*, edited by Hugo Adam Bedau. London and New York: Routledge.

Tachau, Frank, and Metin Heper. 1983. 'The State, Politics, and the Military in Turkey'. *Comparative Politics* 16 (1): 17–33.

Takemura, Hitomi, ed. 2009. *International Human Right to Conscientious Objection to Military Service and Individual Duties to Disobey Manifestly Illegal Orders*. Berlin and Heidelberg: Springer. <http://link.springer.com/10.1007/978-3-540-70527-7> (last accessed 3 January 2022).

Taylor, Paul M. 2005. *Freedom of Religion: UN and European Human Rights Law and Practice*. Cambridge: Cambridge University Press.

Temperman, Jeroen. 2010. *State-Religion Relationships and Human Rights Law: Towards a Right to Religiously Neutral Governance*. Leiden: M. Nijhoff.

Toker Kılınç, Nilgun. 2009. 'The Morals and Politics of Conscientious Objection, Civil Disobedience and Anti-Militarism'. In *Conscientious Objection: Resisting Militarized Society*, edited by Özgür Heval Çınar and Coşkun Üsterci, 61–73. New York and London: Zed Books.

Turan, Ilter. 1997. 'The Military in Turkish Politics'. *Mediterranean Politics* 2 (2): 123–35.

Üçpınar, Hülya. 2009. 'The Criminality of Conscientious Objection in Turkey and Its Consequences'. In *Conscientious Objection: Resisting Militarized Society*, edited by Özgür Heval Çınar and Coşkun Üsterci. New York and London: Zed Books.

United Nations Commission on Human Rights. 1987. 'Conscientious Objection to Military Service (10 March 1987) E/CN.4/RES/1987/46'. <http://www.refworld.org/docid/3b00f0ce50.html> (last accessed 21 May 2017).

United Nations Human Rights Committee (HRC). 1993. 'CCPR General Comment No. 22: Article 18 (Freedom of Thought, Conscience or Religion), 30 July 1993,

CCPR/C/21/Rev.1/Add.4'. <http://www.refworld.org/docid/453883fb22.html> (last accessed 14 April 2017).

United Nations Human Rights Committee. 2012. 'Concluding Observations on the Initial Report of Turkey Adopted by the Committee at Its 106th Session 15 October to 2 November (13 November 2012) CCPR/C/TUR/CO/1'.

United Nations Human Rights Committee. n.d. 'General Comment No. 32, Article 14 Right to Equality before Courts and Tribunals and to Fair Trial (23 August 2007) CCPR/C/GC/32'. (last accessed 24 July 2017).

United Nations Working Group on Arbitrary Detention. n.d. 'Recommendation 2: Detention of Conscientious Objectors E/CN.4/2001/14'.

Urhan, Betül, and Seydi Çelik. 2010. 'Perceptions of "National Security" in Turkey and Their Impacts on the Labor Movement and Trade Union Activities'. *European Journal of Turkish Studies. Social Sciences on Contemporary Turkey* 11.

Üsterci, Coskun, and Ugur Yorulmaz. 2009. 'Conscientious Objection in Turkey'. In *Conscientious Objection: Resisting Militarized Society*, edited by Özgür Heval Çınar and Coşkun Üsterci. New York and London: Zed Books.

Ustun, Cigdem, and Ozgehan Senyuva. 2013. 'Turkish Political Elite Perceptions on Security'. In *Debating Security in Turkey: Challenges and Changes in the Twenty-first Century*, edited by Ebru Canan-Sokullu, 271. Lanham, MD: Lexington Books.

Voorhoof, Dirk. 2009. 'Freedom of Expression under the European Human Rights System – From Sunday Times (No 1) v. U.K. (1979) to Hachette Filipacchi Associes (Ici Paris) v. France (2009)'. *Inter-American and European Human Rights Journal* 2: 3.

Voorhoof, Dirk, and Hannes Cannie. 2010. 'Freedom of Expression and Information in a Democratic Society: The Added but Fragile Value of the European Convention on Human Rights'. *International Communication Gazette* 72 (4–5): 407–23. <https://doi.org/10.1177/1748048510362711> (last accessed 3 January 2022).

Walzer, Michael. 1970. *Obligations; Essays on Disobedience, War, and Citizenship.* Cambridge, MA: Harvard University Press.

Weissbrodt, D. 1988. 'The United Nations Commission on Human Rights Confirms Conscientious Objection to Military Service as a Human Right'. *Netherlands International Law Review* 35 (1): 53–72.

Whitworth, Sandra. 2004. *Men, Militarism, and UN Peacekeeping: A Gendered Analysis.* Boulder, CO: Lynne Rienner.

Wolff, Russell. 1982. 'Conscientious Objection: Time for Recognition as a Fundamental Human Right'. *ASILS Int'l L.J.* 6 (65): 65–95.

Woodward, Rachel, and Trish Winter. 2007. *Sexing the Soldier: The Politics of Gender and the Contemporary British Army.* London and New York: Routledge.

Yesil, Bilge. 2004. '"Who Said This Is a Man's War?": Propaganda, Advertising Discourse and the Representation of War Worker Women during the Second World War'. *Media History* 10 (2): 103–17. <https://doi.org/10.1080/136888004 2000254838> (last accessed 3 January 2022).

Yildirim, Mine. 2010. 'Conscientious Objection to Military Service: International Human Rights Law and the Case of Turkey'. *Religion & Human Rights* 5 (1): 65–91.

Yildirim, Mine. 2012. 'Turkey: Selective Progress on Conscientious Objection'. Forum 18 News Service. 1 May. <http://www.forum18.org/archive.php?article_id=1696&layout_type=mobile> (last accessed 3 January 2022).

Yıldırım, Mine, and Hülya Üçpınar. 2021. 'Conscientious Objection to Military Service in Turkey'. Association for Conscientious Objection. <https://drive.google.com/file/d/1OgQUzlHlEhMWZ_RfLfZRVnoniOo5_aIw/view> (last accessed 18 January 2022).

Accessed on 18.01.2022

Yin, Robert K. 1994. *Case Study Research: Design and Methods*. London and Thousand Oaks, CA: Sage.

Yuval-Davis, Nira. 1997. *Gender & Nation*. Politics and Culture. London and Thousand Oaks, CA: Sage.

Zeiger, Susan. 1996. 'She Didn't Raise Her Boy to Be a Slacker: Motherhood, Conscription, and the Culture of the First World War'. *Feminist Studies* 22 (1): 6. <https://doi.org/10.2307/3178245> (last accessed 3 January 2022).

Zürcher, Erik Jan. 2009. 'Refusing to Serve by Other Means: Desertion in the Late Ottoman Empire'. In *Conscientious Objection: Resisting Militarized Society*, edited by Özgür Heval Çınar and Coşkun Üsterci, 45–52. New York and London: Zed Books.

INDEX

EU representative:
Easy Access System Europe
Mustamäe tee 50, 10621 Tallinn, Estonia
Gpsr.requests@easproject.com

www.ingramcontent.com/pod-product-compliance
Lightning Source LLC
Chambersburg PA
CBHW071745270326
41928CB00013B/2803